ANNOTATED BIBLIOGRAPHY OF PHYTOCHEMICALS

ANNOTATED BIBLIOGRAPHY OF PHYTOCHEMICALS

Dr. Amritpal Singh

HERBAL CONSULTANT

SCIENTIFIC PUBLISHERS (INDIA)

P.O. Box 91 JODHPUR

Published by:
Pawan Kumar Sharma
Scientific Publishers (India)
5-A, New Pali Road, P.O. Box 91
Jodhpur – 342 001 (India)
Tel.: +91-291-2433323
Fax.: +91-291-2512580
E-mail: info@scientificpub.com

ISBN: 81-7233-449-4

Laser typeset : Vijendra Singh
Printed in India

PREFACE

Medicinal plants have been used for curing and preventing diseases since ancient times. Medicinal plants were processed in various forms like : decoction, infusion, powder and tinctures for therapeutic effects. These preparations were however crude and gradually replaced by extracts. Extracts are concentrated preparations and more potential medicinal agents. Today, we have standardized extracts available with us, which provide definite amount of active constituent. Today, for majority of the medicinal plants, active constituents have been traced and applied for further research.

Keeping in mind the growing importance of phytochemical (phyto refers to plant and chemical to constituent), it has become essential to collect the scattered information. The work titled "Annotated Bibliography of Phytochemicals" is an attempt directed to this aim. The phytochemicals have been arranged according to natural order (family) and there biological source and pharmacological effect mentioned followed by references. Majority of the phytochemicals mentioned in the text are novel, although, some old one has been retained because of their historical and everlasting significance. Also, index of phytochemicals studied in this book has been given after text matter — it will assist to readers in tracing out the desired plant constituents.

We hope, that, the work will useful for academicians and persons involved in medicinal plant research. Further, the work will be useful for students of alternative system of healings like Ayurveda, Siddha, Unanai, Traditional Chinese Medicine (TCM) and Western Medicinal Herbalism. We have tried to include accurate information in the text but, still some mistakes may creep in. We appeal to the potential readers to bring mistakes in our notice, so that, they can be rectified. We also invite suggestions for further improvement of the book. Lastly, I extend my sincere thanks to Mr. Pawan Kumar (Scientific Publishers (India)), for bringing out this work.

Dr. Amritpal Singh

2101, Ph. – 7, Mohali
S.A.S. Nagar (Distt. Ropar)

CONTENTS

FAMILIES **Page No.**

PHYTOCHEMICALS STUDIED IN ANGIOSPERMS

The phytochemicals have been arranged according to natural order (family) and their biologically source and pharmacological effect mentioned followed by references. Majority of the phytochemicals mentioned in the text are novel, although, some old one had been retained because of their historical and everlasting significance. The students of alternative system of healings will find this work useful for them.

1. RANUNCULACEAE

6, 7 – dimethoxy - 1, 2, 3, 4 – tetrahydroisoquinoline — Alkaloid present in *Thalictrum lucidum*. It is reported to be antihypertensive.

Wu WN *et al., Lloydia*. 1976. 39(4) : 204 - 12.

8 – acetylcondelphine — Alkaloid present in *Delphinium pyrimadale.*

14 – demethylugaconitine — Norditerpenoid alkaloid present in *Delphinium stapeliosum.*

14 – deacetyl – 14 – isobutyrylnudicauline — Norditerpenoid alkaloid present in *Delphinium stapeliosum.*

15 – alpha hydroxyneoline — Alkaloid present in *Aconitum napellus* and *Aconitum jaluense.*

Shim S.H. *Arch. Pharm. Res. Vol. 26,* No. 9, 709 - 715, 2003.

27 – deoxyactein — Xyloside present in *Cimcifuga racemosa*

Mamta, T.; Shukla, Y.N.; Tandon, M. *Current Research on Medicinal and Aromatic Plants*. 1995, 17 : 2, 202 - 210; 45 ref.

Actein — Xyloside present in *Cimcifuga racemosa.*

Acolyctine — Alkaloid present in *Aconitum lycoctonum.*

Aconasutine — Alkaloid present in *Aconitum nasutum.*

Aconine — Alkaloid present in *Aconitum ferox.*

Aconitine — Alkaloid present in *Aconitum ferox.*

Alder Wright, Reports on Aconite Alkaloids.

Ameri A., Shi Q., Peters T. (1995) *Naunyn - Schmiedeberg's Arch. Pharmacol.* (Suppl.) 351 : R650.

Chan, T.Y.K., *Hum. Exp Toxicol* 1994; 36 : 326 - 8.

D-F Yeih, F-T Chiang, S.K.S. Huang. *Heart* 2000; 84 : e8 (October).

Fluckiger, *Archiv present in Pharm.* B.191, P.196.

Groves, *Pha. Jour and Trans.* 1873 - 74, P. 293.

M.R.Riva, B.Brando. Institute present in Pharmacological Sciences, University present in Milan, Italy.

Peper, K,. Trautwein, W. *Pflugers Arch Gesamte Physiol Menschen Tiere.* 1967; 296(4) : 328 – 336.

Rep. Chem. Exam for Bengal, 1885.

Saresella, M. *et al.*, Roda, K., Speciale, L., Tramelli, D., Guerini, F., Ferrante, P. *J. Immunol Methods* 1997; 210; 227 - 34.

The Alkaloids, Vol. 1, R.H.F. Manske Ed., (Academic Press New York) (1950). 33 - 206.

Aonidin — Glucoside present in *Adonis versalis.*

Adadine — Alkaloid present in *Consolida ambigua.*

Adonitoxin — Steroid glycoside present in *Adonis versalis.* It is cardiac tonic.

Ajacine — Norditerpenoid alkaloid present in *Delphinium stapeliosum.*

Ajacusine — Alkaloid present in *Consolida ambigua.*

Ajadine — Norditerpenoid alkaloid present in *Delphinium stapeliosum.*

Ambiguine — Alkaloid present in *Consolida ambigua.*

Atidine — Alkaloid present in *Aconitum heterophyllum.*

Atisenol — Entatisene diterpenoid lactone present in *Aconitum heterophyllum.*

Atisine — Alkaloid present in *Aconitum heterophyllum.*

Dzhakhangirov, F.N.; Bessonova, I.A. *Chemistry of Natural Compounds*, Volume 38, Number 1, 2002, pp. 74 - 77(4).

Avadharidine — Alkaloid present in *Aconitum erectum.*

Barbinine — Alkaloid present in *Delphinium* spp.

Dobelis, P. *Pharmacology and Experimental Therapeutics*. Vol. 291, Issue 2, 538 - 546, 1999.

Beiwutine — Alkaloid present in *Aconitum pulcherrimum.*

Berberine — Alkaloid present in *Hydrastis canadensis* and *Thalictrum foliosum.*

Bikhaconitine — Alkaloid present in *Aconitum falconeri, Aconitum ferox, Aconitum spicatum, Aconitum patentipilum* and *Aconitum violaceum.*

Browniine — Alkaloid present in *Delphinium brownii.*

Aiyar, V. *et al.*, 1978. The alkaloids present in *Delphinium brownii*. *Phytochemistry*. 17 : 1453 – 1454.

Benn, M.H., M.A.M. Cameron, and O.E. Edwards. 1963. *Can. J. Chem*. 41 : 477 – 482.

Caltholid — Triterpene lactone present in *Caltha palustris.*

Cathine — Alkaloid present in *Caltha edulis.*

Schechter, MD. *Pharmacol Biochem Behav.* 1990. 36(4) : 817-20.

Cathionine — Alkaloid present in *Caltha edulis.*

Schechter, MD. *Pharmacol Biochem Behav.* 1990. 36(4) : 817-20.

Celliamine — Alkaloid present in *Helleborus niger.*

Chasmaconitine — Alkaloid present in *Aconitum chasmanthum.*

Chasmanthinine — Alkaloid present in *Aconitum chasmanthum.*

Cimcifugin — Neutral principle present in *Cimcifuga racemosa.*

Cimicifugoside — Xyloside present in *Cimcifuga racemosa.*

Columbamine — Alkaloid present in *Thalictrum lucidum.* It is reported to be antihypertensive and and antibacterial.

Wu WN et al., *Lloydia.* 1976. 39(4) : 204 - 12.

Condelphine — Alkaloid present in *Delphinium pyrimadale.*

Coptine — Alkaloid present in *Coptis chinensis* and *Coptis teeta.*

Trans. present in Med. and Phys.Soc present in Calcutta, Vol.VII1. 85.

Prpresent in. Simpson *Phar. Jour.* 1854, Vol. X111., p.413.

Crassicauline — Alkaloid present in *Aconitum patentipilum.*

Cymarin — Steroid glycoside present in *Adonis versalis.* It is reported to be cardiac tonic.

Damascenine — Alkaloid present in *Nigella damascene.*

Deboline — Norditerpenoid alkaloid present in *Delphinium stapeliosum.*

Delbruninol — Alkaloid present in *Delphinium brunonianum.*

Delcosine — Norditerpenoid alkaloid present in *Delphinium stapeliosum.*

Delphinine — Alkaloid present in *Delphinium staphistagra.* The alkaloid is antidote to digoxin and muscarine poisoning.

Alkaloid present in *Delphinium* spp.

Dobelis, P. *Pharmacology and Experimental Therapeutics.* Vol. 291, Issue 2, 538 – 546. 1999.

Deltatsine — Norditerpenoid alkaloid present in *Delphinium stapeliosum.*

Deoxyacetylacteol — Xyloside present in *Cimcifuga racemosa.*

Dihydroajaconine — Alkaloid present in *Consolida ambigua.*

F - dihydroatisine — Alkaloid present in *Aconitum heterophyllum.*

Franchetine — Alkaloid present in *Aconitum patentipilum.*

F. Wang, Z. Li, X. Dai, C. Peng. *Phytochemistry* 45(7) (1997) pp. 1539-1542.

Helleborine — Alkaloid present in *Helleborus niger.*

Heteratisine — Alkaloid present in *Aconitum heterophyllum.*

Heterophylisine — Alkaloid present in *Aconitum heterophyllum.*

Heterophyllidine — Alkaloid present in *Aconitum heterophyllum.*

Heterophylline — Alkaloid present in *Aconitum heterophyllum.*

Hetidine — Alkaloid present in *Aconitum heterophyllum.*

Hetisine — Alkaloid present in *Aconitum heterophyllum.*

Higenamine — Alkaloid present in *Aconitum napellus.* It is reported to be antiarrhythmic.

Yu., G.R. *et al.*, *Acta Cardiol.* 1985. 40(4) : 409 - 20.

Kimura, I. *et al.*, *Jpn J Pharmacol.* 1994. 66(1) : 75 - 80.

Hokbusine - A — Alkaloid present in *Aconitum napellus and Aconitum jaluense.*

Shim, S.H. *Arch Pharm Res* Vol. 26, No. 9, 709 - 715, 2003.

Homoaromoline — Alkaloid present in *Thalictrum lucidum.* It is reportd to be antihypertensive.

Wu., W.N. *et al.*, *Lloydia.* 1976. 39(4) : 204 - 12.

Hydrastine — Alkaloid present in *Hydrastis canadensis.* It is reported to be gabaergic antagonist.

Hypaconitine — Alkaloid present in *Aconitum napellus* and *Aconitum jaluense.* It is highly poisonous.

Liu., H. and Katz, A. In : *PM* 62(2) : 190 - 191. 1997.

Shim, S.H. *Arch Pharm Res* Vol. 26, No. 9, 709 - 715, 2003.

Indaconitine — Alkaloid present in *Aconitum chasmanthum* and *m ferox.*

Isoatisine — Alkaloid present in *Aconitum heterophyllum.*

Isotalatizidine — Alkaloid present in *Delphinium pyrimadale.*

Jatrorrhizine — Alkaloid present in *Thalictrum lucidum.* It is reported to be antihypertensive and antibacterial.

Wu, W.N., Beal, J.L., Mitscher, L.A., Salman, K.N., Patil, P. *Lloydia.* 1976. 39(4) : 204 - 12.

Jesaconitine — Alkaloid present in *Aconitum napellus.*

Liu, H. and Katz, A. In : *PM* 62(2) : 190 - 191. 1997.

K - strophanthoside — Steroid glycoside present in *Adonis versalis.* It is reported to be cardiac tonic.

Lapoaconitine — Alkaloid present in *Aconitum leave.*

Lipomesaconitine — Alkaloid present in *Aconitum napellus and Aconitum jaluense.*

Liu, H. and Katz, A. In : *PM* 62(2) : 190 - 191. 1997.

Shim, S.H. *Arch. Pharm. Res. Vol.* 26, No. 9, 709 - 715, 2003.

Lycaconitine — Alkaloid present in *Aconitum lycoctonum.*

Melathin — Saponin present in *Nigella sativa.*

Mesaconitine (N - desethyl - N - methylaconitine) — Alkaloid present in *Aconitum napellus.*

Angela Ameri. *British Journal present in Pharmacology* (1998) 123, 243 – 250.

Mithaconitine — Alkaloid present in *Aconitum falconeri.*

Napelline — Alkaloid present in *Aconitum napellus.*

Nigellidine — Alkaloid present in *Nigella sativa.*

Nigellin — Bitter principle present in *Nigella sativa.*

Nudicauline — Norditerpenoid alkaloid present in *Delphinium stapeliosum.*

Obaberine — Alkaloid present in *Thalictrum lucidum.* It is reported to be antihypertensive.

Wu, W.N., Beal, J.L., Mitscher, L.A., Salman, K.N., Patil, P. *Lloydia*. 1976. 39(4) : 204 - 12.

bamegine — Alkaloid present in *Thalictrum lucidum*. It is ported to be antihypertensive.

Wu, W.N. *et al*., *Lloydia*. 1976. 39(4) : 204 - 12.

- methyl - thalicberine — Alkaloid present in *Thalictrum cidum*. It is reported to be antihypertensive.

Wu, W.N. *et al*., *Lloydia*. 1976. 39(4) : 204 - 12.

litoriside — Cardiac glycoside present in *Adonis magnolica*. It is eart tonic. It is also present in *Cochorus olitorius*.

Smailova, R.D. *Vrach Delo*. 1981. (8) : 21 - 2.

Soerenby, L. & Lindhale, P.E. *Farmakol Toksikol*. 1964. 27 : 48-53

xaconitine — Alkaloid present in *Aconitum napellus*.

Liu, H. and Katz, A. In : *PM* 62(2) : 190 - 191. 1997.

xyberberine — Alkaloid present in *Thalictrum lucidum*. It is eported to be antihypertensive.

Wu, W.N. *et al*., *Lloydia*. 1976. 39(4) : 204 - 12.

almatisine — Diterpene alkaloid present in *Aconitum palmatum*.

alustrolid — Triterpene lactone present in *Caltha palustris*.

rotoanemonine — Glucoside present in *Ranunculus scelretus*.

enbusine - C — Alkaloid present in *Delphinium pyrimadale*.

eptentriodine — Alkaloid present in *Aconitum erectum*.

prinitallamine — Alkaloid present in *Helleborus niger*. It is eported to be toxic.

Naunyn, A. Schiedeberg's. *Archiv fuer Experimentelle Pathologie and Pharmakologie*. 110 - 253, 1925 - 66.

printilline — Alkaloid present in *Helleborus niger*.

taphisagrine — Alkaloid present in *Delphinium denudatum*.

halictrine — Alkaloid present in *Thalictrum simplex*.

Umarov, S. *et al.*, *Chemistry of Natural Compounds*.Vol. 4(5) 280, 1971.

Thalictrine — Alkaloid present in *Thalictrum simplex.*

Thalidomide — Alkaloid present in *Thalictrum lucidum.* It reported to be antihypertensive.

Wu, W.N., Beal, J.L., Mitscher, L.A., Salman, K.N., Patil, *Lloydia*. 1976. 39(4) : 204 - 12.

Thalifebridine — Alkaloid present in *Thalictrum faberi.* It reported to be cytotoxic.

Thalifendine — Alkaloid present in *Thalictrum lucidum.* It reported to be antihypertensive.

Wu, W.N. *et al.*, *Lloydia*. 1976. 39(4) : 204 - 12.

Thaliglucinone — Alkaloid present in *Thalictrum lucidum.* It reported to be antihypertensive.

Wu, W.N. *et al.*, *Lloydia*. 1976. 39(4) : 204 - 12.

Thalrugosine — Alkaloid present in *Thalictrum lucidum.* It reported to be antihypertensive.

Wu, W.N. *et al.*, *Lloydia*. 1976. 39(4) : 204 - 12.

Triloquinine — Cyanogenic glycoside present in *Aquilegia vulgaris*

Vilmorisine — Alkaloid present in *Aconitum patentipilum.*

F. Wang, Z. Li, X. Dai, C. Peng. *Phytochemistry* 45 (7) (1997) p 1539 - 1542.

Xanthopuccine — Alkaloid present in *Hydrastis canadensis.*

Yunaconitine — Alkaloid present in *Aconitum patentipilum.*

2. MAGNOLIACEAE

Liriodendron — Lignan present in *Liriodendron tulipifera.*

Shikimic acid — Organic acid present in *Illicium verum.*

Tulipiferine — Alkaloid present in *Liriodendron tulipifera.*

Shizandrin — Flavonoids present in *Schizandra grandiflora.*

3. ANNONACEAE

nnomonsyvin — Acetogenin present in *Annona montana*. It is totoxic.

Jossang, A., *et al*. *J. Nat. Prod.* 1991; 54(4) : 967 - 71.

nnomuricin – E — Acetogenin present in *Annona montana*.

Kim, G. S., *et al*. *J. Nat. Prod.* 1998; 61(4) : 432 - 436.

nnomuricinine — Alkaloid present in *Annona muricata*.

nnonacin — Acetogenin present in *Annona montana*. It is reported be cytotoxic.

Lannuzel, A., *et al*. *Neuroscience* 2003; 121(2) : 287 - 296.

Yuan, Shyng-Shiou F., *et al*. *Life Sciences* 2003; 72 : 2853 - 2861.

nnonaine — Alkaloid present in *Annona muricata*.

ntioquine — Alkaloid present in *Pseudoxandra sclerocarpa*. It is ported to be calcium antagonist.

D'Ocon, M.P. *et al*., *Arch Int Pharmacodyn Ther*. 1989. 297 : 205 - 16.

therosperminine — Alkaloid present in *Annona muricata*.

anangine — Alkaloid present in *Cleistopholis patens*.

Leboeuf, M. and Cave, A. *Lloydia*. 1976. 39(6) : 459 - 60.

rebanin — Alkaloid present in *Fissistigma glaucescens*.

Lo, W.L. *et al*., *Journal present in Chinese Chemical Society*, 2000, 47, 1251 - 1256.

upolauridine — Alkaloid present in *Cleistopholis patens*. It is ntifungal.

Khan, S.I. *Antimicrob Agents Chemother*. 2002. 46(6) : 1785-92.

igantetronenin — Acetogenin present in *Goniothalamus ganteus*. It is reported to be cytotoxic.

Fang, X. P., *et al*. *J. Nat. Prod.* 1992; 55(11) : 1655 - 63.

igantrionenin — Acetogenin present in *Goniothalamus giganteus*. is cytotoxic.

Fang, X. P., *et al. J. Nat. Prod.* 1992; 55(11) : 1655 - 63.

Jatrorrhizine — Protoberberine alkaloid present in *Enan chlorantha.*

Virtanen, P. *et al., Acta Anat* (Basel). 1988; 131(2) : 166 - 70.

Liriodenine — Alkaloid present in *Fissistigma glaucescens.* It reported to be muscarinic receptor antagonist and antiprotozoal.

Lin, C.H. *et al., Br. J. Pharmacol.* 1994. 113(1) : 275 - 81.

Waechter, A.I. *et* al., *Phytotherpy Research*, 1999. 13(2) : 175 - 17

Melosmine — Alkaloid present in *Guatteria melosma*

Zabel, V., *et al., J. Nat. Prods.* 45 : 94.

Melosmidine — Alkaloid present in *Guatteria melosma.*

Zabel, V., *et al., J. Nat. Prods.* 45 : 94.

Muricapentocin — Acetogenin present in *Annona montana.*

Kim, G. S., *et al. J. Nat. Prod.* 1998; 61(4) : 432 - 436.

Norannuradhapurine — Alkaloid present in *Fissistigma glauce-scen*

Lo, W.L. *et al., Journal present in Chinese Chemical Socie* 2000, 47, 1251 - 1256.

Oxoanolobine — Alkaloid present in *Guatteria melosma.*

Phoebe, C.H. *et al., Heterocycles* 14 : 1977.

Xylopine — Alkaloid present in *Fissistigma glaucescens* (Annonaceae)

Lo, W.L. *et al., Journal present in Chinese Chemical Socie* 2000, 47, 1251 - 1256.

4. MENISPERMACEAE

Berberine — Alkaloid present in *Tinospora cordifolia.*

Calumbin — Bitter principle present in *Tinospora cordifolia.*

Carococculine — Alkaloid present in *Cocculus carolinus.*

Slatkin, D.J. *et al.,* 1974. *Lloydia* 37 : 1974.

Cissamine — Alkaloid present in *Cissampelos pariera.*

Cissampareine — Alkaloid present in *Cissampelos pariera*.

Coccoline — Alkaloid present in *Cocculus laurifolius*.

Cocculidine — Alkaloid present in *Cocculus laurifolius*.

Cocculine — Alkaloid present in *Cocculus laurifolius*.

Cocculitine — Alkaloid present in *Cocculus laurifolius*.

Coccuvine — Alkaloid present in *Cocculus laurifolius*.

Coclaurine — Alkaloid present in *Cocculus laurifolius*.

Coscoline — Alkaloid present in *Cocculus laurifolius*.

Cosculine — Alkaloid present in *Cocculus laurifolius*.

Cosculinine — Alkaloid present in *Cocculus laurifolius*.

Cuspidaline — Bisbenzylisoquinoline alkaloid present in *Limacia cuspidate*.

Tomita, M. *et al.*, *Yakugaku Zasshi*. 1967. 87(7) : 793 - 6.

Cuspidaline — Bisbenzylisoquinoline alkaloid present in *Limacia cuspidata*.

Tomitab, M. *et al.*, *Yakugaku Zasshi*. 1967. 87(7) : 793 - 6.

Cyclanoline — Alkaloid present in *Cissampelos pariera*.

Cycleanine — Alkaloid present in *Cissampelos pariera*.

Alkaloid present in *Tiliacora dinklagei*.

Dwuma - Badu, D., *et al.*, *The Journal of Natural Products* 39 : 213.

Funiferine — Biphenyl alkaloid present in *Tiliacora funifera*.

Tackie, A.N., D. Dwuma - Badu, J.E. Knapp and P.L. Schiff, Jr. 1972. *Lloydia* 36 : 66.

Giloin — Glucoside present in *Tinospora cordifolia*.

Hayatidine — Alkaloid present in *Cissampelos pariera*.

Hayatine — Alkaloid present in *Cissampelos pariera*.

Hayatinine — Alkaloid present in *Cissampelos pariera*.

Insularine — Bisbenzoylisoquinoline alkaloid present in *Cissampelos pariera*. It is reported to be antiameobic and cytotoxic.

Marshall, S.J. *et al. Antimicrobial Agents and Chemotherapy*, 01 1994, 96 - 103, Vol. 38, No. 1.

Isochondodendrine — Alkaloid present in *Cissampelos pariera.*

Jateorhizine — Alkaloid present in *Cocculus palmatus.*

Laurifine — Aporphine alkaloid present in *Cocculus laurifolius.*

Laurifinine — Aporphine alkaloid present in *Cocculus laurifolius.*

Laurifonine — Aporphine alkaloid present in *Cocculus laurifolius.*

Laurifoline — Aporphine alkaloid present in *Cocculus laurifolius.*

Limacine — Bisbenzylisoquinoline alkaloid present in *Limacia cuspidate.*

Tomita, M. *et al.*, *Yakugaku Zasshi.* 1967. 87(7) : 793 - 6.

Limacusine — Bisbenzylisoquinoline alkaloid present in *Limacia cuspidate.*

Tomita, M. *et al.*, *Yakugaku Zasshi.* 1967. 87(7) : 793 - 6.

Menismine — Alkaloid present in *Cissamparelos pariera.*

Menispermine — Alkaloid present in *Anamirta paniculata.*

Microphyllone — Prenylbenoquinone present in *Ehretia microphylla.* It is reported to be antiallergic and antidiabetic.

Yamaura, S. *et al.*, *Phytochemistry.* 1995. 39(1) : 105 - 10.

Nortiliacorinine - A — Alkaloid present in *Tiliacora funifera.*

Tackie, A.N., *et al.*, *Phytochemistry* 12 : 203.

Oblongine — Alkaloid present in *Tiliacora funifera.*

Tackie, A.N.,*et al.*, *Phytochemistry* 19 : 1882.

Parierine — Alkaloid present in *Cissampelos pariera.*

Pelosine — Alkaloid present in *Cissampelos pareira.*

Phaeanthine — Alkaloid present in *Cyclea burmanni.*

Bandara, B.M.R. *et al.*, In : *Planta Med.*, 56(2) : 1990. 245 - 6.

Picrotoxin — Neutral principle present in *Anamirta paniculata.*

Steapherine — Alkaloid present in *Sarcopetalum harveyanum.*

Sowemimo, B.O. *et al., Lloydia.* 1972. 35(1) : 90 - 1.*

Tiliafunimine — Alkaloid present in *Tiliacora funifera.*

Ayim, J.S.K., *et al., The Journal of Natural Products* 40 : 561.

Tiliageine — Biphenyl alkaloid present in *Tiliacora dinklagei*

Tackie, A.N., *et al., Experientia* 30 : 847.

Tinosporide — Diterpenoid furanolactone present in *Tinospora cordifolia.*

K. Swaminathan, *et al., Acta Cryst.* (1989). C45, 134 - 136.

Tinosporinone — Bitter principle present in *Tinospora cordifolia.*

Tridictyophylline — Alkaloid present in *Triclisia dictyophylla.*

Spiff, A.I., *et al., J. Nat. Prod.* 44 : 160.

Trigilletimine — Alkaloid present in *Triclisia* spp.

Schiff, Jr. 1975. *Experientia* 31 : 1251.

5. BERBERIDACAE

Berbamine — Alkaloid present in *Berberis aristata.*

Stille and Maisch. *Nat. Disp.*, 3rd Ed., p.315.

Berberine — Alkaloid present in *Berberis aristata, Berberis aquifolium* and *Berberis lycium.* It is reported to be antibacterial, anti-inflammatory, cytotoxic and antimutagenic.

Fuduka, K. *et al., Journal present in Ethnopharmacology*, Vol. 66 (2) : p. 227 - 233. 1999.

Iwasa, K. *et al., Planta Med* 1997, 63 : 196 - 198.

Kuo, C.L., Chou, C.C., Yung, B.Y.M., *Cancer Letters* 1995, 93 : 193 - 200.

Lahiri, S.C. and N.K. Dutta (1967) - *Journal of the Indian Medical Association* 48, 1.

Marta Cernakova, *et al., B.MC. Complementary and Alternative Medicine.* 2002. 2 : 2.

W.H. Perkin, jun., *Journ. Chem. Soc.* Feb., 1996.

Caulophyllin — Alkaloid present in *Caulophyllum thalicotroides.*

Icariin — Flavonol glycoside present in *Epimedium koreanum*. It is reported to be aphrodisiac and antihepatotoxic.

Du, Q., Xia, M., Ito, Y. *J. Chromatogr A.* 2002; 962 : 239 - 41.

Lee, M.K. *et al., Planta Med.* 1995; 61 : 523 - 6.

Fu, J. *et al., Chinese Pharmacological Bulletin* 2002; 18 : 430 - 2.

ZC, Xin., *et al., Asian J. Androl* 2003 Mar; 5 : 15 - 18.

Nantenine — Aporphine alkaloid present in *Nandina domestica.* It is reported to be anticonvulsant, antihypertensive (calcium channel blocker) and 3,4-methylenedioxymethamphetamine (MDMA) antagonist.

Fantegrosii, F.E. *et al., Psychopharmacology* (Berl). 2004. 22.

Orallo, F. *Planta Medica.* 2004. 70(2) : 117 - 126.

Riberio, R.A. *et al., Phytomedicine.* 2001. 8(2) : 107 - 11.

Oblongine — Alkaloid of *Leontice lentopetalum.*

Abdalla, S. *et al.*, Phytotherapy Research, Vol. 9(1) :p. 60 - 63, 1995

Oxycanthine — Alkaloid present in *Berberis aristata.*

Podophyllin — Resin present in *Podophyllum hexandrum.*

Kumar, B.; and Murlidhar, S. *Indian Journal present in Sexually Transmitted Diseases.* Vol. 19 (2) : p.99 - 101, 1988.

Podophyllotoxin — Resin present in *Podophyllum hexandrum.* Paint of the drug is applied on the warts.

Kumar, B.; and Murlidhar, S. *Indian Journal present in Sexually Transmitted Diseases.* Vol. 19 (2) : p.99 - 101, 1988.

Pyncamine — Alkaloid present in *Pycnarrhena manillensis.*

Bruchhausen von *et al., Arch Pharm.* 1960. 293 / 65 : 454 - 61.

6. NYMPHAEACEAE

Armepavine — Isoquinoline alkaloid present in *Nelumbo nucifera.*

Asimilobine — Isoquinoline alkaloid present in *Nelumbo nucifera.*

Isoliensinine — Isoquinoline alkaloid present in *Nelumbo nucifera.*

Liensinine — Isoquinoline alkaloid present in *Nelumbo nucifera.*

Lotusine — Isoquinoline alkaloid present in *Nelumbo nucifera.*

Neferine — Isoquinoline alkaloid present in *Nelumbo nucifera.*

Nelumbine — Isoquinoline alkaloid present in *Nelumbo nucifera.*

N - norarmepavine — Isoquinoline alkaloid present in *Nelumbo nucifera.*

Nornuciferine — Isoquinoline alkaloid present in *Nelumbo nucifera.*

Nuciferine — Isoquinoline alkaloid present in *Nelumbo nucifera.*

Oxoushinsunine — Isoquinoline alkaloid present in *Nelumbo nucifera.*

Roemerin — Isoquinoline alkaloid present in *Nelumbo nucifera.*

7. PAPAVERACEAE

(-) - **flavinantine** — Alkaloid present in *Meconopsis cambrica.*

Jiri SLAVIK and Leonora SLAVIKOVA. *Collection present in Czechoslovak Chemical Communications.* Abstracts: 1996, 61(12) : 1815 - 1822.

(+) - **Bublocapnine** — Isoquinoline alkaloid present in *Corydalis cava* and *Glaucium fimbrilligerum.* It is reported to be anticonvulsant and antinociceptive.

Shin, J.S. *et al., Neurosci Lett.* 1998. 20; 244(3) : 161 - 4.

R.A. Hahn, *et al., Pharmacology and Experimental Therapeutics.* 1982. 1; 223(2) : 305 - 313.

Z. Mahmoudi, A. Shafiee. *ISHS Acta Horticulturae* 333: WOCMAP I - Medicinal and Aromatic Plants Conference : part 1 present in 4.

Zetler, G. *Arch. Int. Pharmacodyn Ther.* 1988. 296 : 255 - 81.

(+) - **corytuberine** — Isoquinoline alkaloid present in *Corydalis cava* and *Meconopsis cambrica.*

Zetler, G. *Arch. Int. Pharmacodyn Ther.* 1988. 296 : 255 - 81.

(+) – **mecambroline** — Alkaloid present in *Meconopsis cambrica.*

Jiri SLAVIK and Leonora SLAVIKOVA. *Collection present in Czechoslovak Chemical Communications.* Abstracts: 1996, 61(12), 1815 - 1822.

(+) – **sinactine** — Alkaloid present in *Corydalis meifolia.*

Allocryptopine — Alkaloid present in *Meconopsis cambrica.*

Jiri SLAVIK and Leonora SLAVIKOVA. *Collection present in Czechoslovak Chemical Communications.* Abstracts : 1996, 61(12), 1815 - 1822.

Argemonine — Alkaloid present in *Argemone mexicana.*

Berberine — Alkaloid present in *Argemone mexicana.*

Bicuculline — Alkaloid present in *Corydalis govaniana.* It is convulsant.

Curtiss *et al. Nature* (1970) 226.1222.

Bisnorargemonine — Alkaoid present in *Eschscholzia californica.*

Californidine — Isoquinoline alkaloid present in *Eschscholtzia californica.*

Tome, F., *et al. Phytochemical Analysis.* Vol. 10. Issue 5, p.264-267.

Californine — Isoquinoline alkaloid present in *Eschscholtzia californica.*

Chelamidine — Alkaloid present in *Chelidonium majus.*

Chelamine — Alkaloid present in *Chelidonium majus.*

Cheldiamine — Alkaloid present in *Chelidonium majus.*

Cheilanthifoline — Alkaloid present in *Corydalis meifolia.*

Bhakuni, D.S., Chaturvedi, R. *J. Nat Prod.* 1983. 46(3) : 320 - 4.

Alkaloid present in *Chelidonium majus.*

Chelerythrine — Alkaloid present in *Sanguinaria canadensis.* It is reported to be inhibitor of protein kinase C.

J.M. Herbert, *et al., BBRC* 172, 993 (1990) Abstract.

Chelidonine — Alkaloid present in *Chelidonium majus*. It is reported to be antispasmodic, anticancer and anti-inflammatory.

Hiller, K.O., Ghorbani, M., Schilcher, H. *Planta Med*. 1998; 64 : 758 - 60 [letter].

Hriscu, A., Galesanu, M.R., Moisa, L. *Rev. Med. Chir. Soc. Med. Nat. Lasi*. 1980; 84 : 559 - 61.

Sokolpresent, inf B., Saelhpresent, in C.C., Takeuchi, Y., Powella, R. *Growth* 1964; 28 : 225 - 31.

Vavreckova, C., Gawlik I, Muller K. *Planta Med* 1996; 62:397- 401.

Chelirubine — Alkaloid present in *Eschscholzia californica*.

Chelilutine — Alkaloid present in *Eschscholzia californica*.

Codeine — Alkaloid present in *Papaver somniferum*.

Corlumine — Alkaloid present in *Corydalis meifolia*. It is reported to be antispasmodic.

Bhakuni, D.S., Chaturvedi, R. *J. Nat Prod*. 1983. 46(3) : 320 - 4.

Corycavine — Alkaloid present in *Corydalis tuberosa*.

Pharm., 1908, ccxivi, p. 387.

Corydaline — Alkaloid present in *Corydalis govaniana*.

Rueffer, M., Bauer, W. and Zenk, M.H. *Canad. J. Chem*. 72 (1994) 170 - 175.

Corypalline — Alkaloid present in *Meconopsis cambrica*.

Jiri SLAVIK and Leonora SLAVIKOVA. *Collection present in Czechoslovak Chemical Communications*. Abstracts : 1996, 61(12), 1815 - 1822.

Corysamine — Alkaloid present in *Meconopsis cambrica*.

Jiri SLAVIK and Leonora SLAVIKOVA. *Collection present in Czechoslovak Chemical Communications*. Abstracts: 1996, 61(12), 1815 - 1822.

Cryptocavine — Alkaoid present in *Eschscholzia californica*.

Cularine — Alkaloid present in *Dicentra cucullaria*. It is antispasmodic.

Dehydrocavidine — Alkaloid present in *Corydalis meifolia*. It is antispasmodic.

Bhakuni, D.S., Chaturvedi, R. J. Nat. Prod. 1983. 46(3) : 320 - 4.

Dihydrosanguinarine — Alkaloid present in *Corydalis meifolia*.

Bhakuni, D.S., Chaturvedi, R. J. Nat. Prod. 1983. 46(3) : 320 - 4.

Eschscholzine — Isoquinoline alkaloid present in *Eschscholtzia californica*.

Gindarine — Alkaloid present in *Corydalis aurea* and *Stephania glabra*.

Madan, B.R. *et al., Indian Journal of Pharmacology*. 1974, 6(2) : 97 - 102.

Hunnemanine — Alkaloid present in *Hunnemannia fumarifolia*. It is toxic.

Hydrastine — Alkaloid present in *Corydalis pseudoadunca*. It is reported to be gabaergic antagonist.

Chernevskaja *et al. Toxincon* (1990), 28(6) 727 - 730.

Lauroscholtzine — Alkaoid present in *Eschscholzia californica*.

Mecambridine Alkaloid present in *Meconopsis cambrica*

Jiri SLAVIK and Leonora SLAVIKOVA. *Collection present in Czechoslovak Chemical Communications.* Abstracts : 1996, 61(12) : 1815 - 1822.

Morphine — Alkaloid present in *Papaver somniferum*.

Nantenine — Aporphine alkaloid present in *Platycapnos spicata*. It is reported to be anticonvulsant, antihypertensive (calcium channel blocker) and 3,4-methylenedioxymethamphetamine (MDMA) antagonist.

Fantegrosii, F.E. *et al., Psychopharmacology* (Berl). 2004. 22.

Orallo, F. *Planta Medica*. 2004. 70(2) : 117 - 126.

Riberio, R.A. *et al., Phytomedicine*. 2001 Mar; 8(2) : 107 - 11.

N - methyl - berberine — Alkaloidpresent in *Corydalis longipes*. It is reported to be antifungal.

N - methyl - hernagine — Isoquinoline alkaloid present in *Glaucium fimbrilligerum.*

Z. Mahmoudi, A. Shafiee. ISHS Acta. Horticulturae 333: WOCMAP I - Medicinal and Aromatic Plants Conference: part 1 present in 4.

N - methyl - lindcarpine — Isoquinoline alkaloid present in *Glaucium fimbrilligerum.*

Z. Mahmoudi, A. Shafiee. *ISHS Acta Horticulturae* 333 : WOCMAP I - Medicinal and Aromatic Plants Conference : part 1 present in 4.

Narciene — Alkaloid present in *Papaver somniferum.*

Narcotine — Alkaloid present in *Papaver somniferum.* It is hypnotic.

Noscapine — Alkaloid present in *Papaver somniferum.* It is reported to be antitussive, anticancer and antispasmodic.

Landen, *et al.* (2002). *Cancer Res.* 62 4109.

Mahmoudian and Mojaverian (2001). *Acta. Physiol.* Hung. 88 : 231.

Mourey, *et al.* (1992) *Mol. Pharmacol.* 42 : 619.

Ye. *et al.* (1998). *Proc. Natl. Acad. Sci.* USA 95 : 1601.

Palmatine — Alkaloid present in *Meconopsis cambrica.*

Jiri SLAVIK and Leonora SLAVIKOVA. *Collection present in Czechoslovak Chemical Communications.* Abstracts : 1996, 61(12) : 1815 - 1822.

Papaverine — Alkaloid present in *Papaver somniferum.* It is antispasmodic and aphrodisiac.

Abber, J.C., Lue, T.F., Orvis, B.R., McClure, R.D. and Williams, R.D. (1986). *J. Urol* 135 : 923.

Papaverrubine C — Alkaloid present in *Meconopsis cambrica.*

Jiri SLAVIK and Leonora SLAVIKOVA. *Collection present in Czechoslovak Chemical Communications.* Abstracts: 1996, 61(12) : 1815 - 1822.

Papaverrubine D — Alkaloid present in *Meconopsis cambrica.*

Jiri SLAVIK and Leonora SLAVIKOVA. *Collection present in Czechoslovak Chemical Communications.* Abstracts : 1996, 61(12) : 1815 - 1822.

Parfumidine — Alkaloid present in *Fumaria densiflora.*

Suau, R., *et. al.*, *Phytochem Anal.* 2002. 13(6) : 363 - 7.

Pafrumine — Alkaloid present in *Fumaria densiflora.*

Suau, R., *et. al.*, *Phytochem Anal.* 2002. 13(6) : 363 - 7.

Pocavidine — Alkaloid present in *Corydalis meifolia.*

Bhakuni, D.S., Chaturvedi, R. *J. Nat. Prod.* 1983. 46(3) : 320 - 4.

Porphyroxine — Alkaloid present in *Papaver somniferum.*

Brochmann-Hanseen, E. and Hirari, K. Opium alkaloids. V. *J. Pharm Sci.* 1967. 56(12) : 1658 - 60.

Protopine — Alkaloid present in *Argemone mexicana* and *Papaver somniferum.* It is reported to be calcium channel blocker and antiplatelet agent.

Pseudomorphine — Alkaloid present in *Papaver somniferum.*

Rhoeadine — Alkaloid present in *Papaver rhoeas.*

Rhoeagenine — Alkaloid present in *Papaver rhoeas.*

Ribasine — Alkaloid present in *Corydalis claviculata* and *Sarcocapnos crassifolia.*

Roemeroline — Alkaloid present in *Meconopsis cambrica.*

Jiri SLAVIK and Leonora SLAVIKOVA. *Collection present in Czechoslovak Chemical Communications.* Abstracts : 1996, 61(12) : 1815 - 1822.

Rotundine — It is L-optical isomer present in tetrahydropalmatine. It is reported to be analgesic, dopamine - 2 - receptor blocker, sedative and tran-quillizer.

Salutaridine — Isoquinoline alkaloid present in *Glaucium fimbrilligerum* and *Nandina domestica.*

Kardos, J., Blasko, G., Simonyi, M., Szantay, C. *Arzneimittel-forschung.* 1984; 34(12) : 1758 - 9.

Sangunarine — Alkaloid present in *Sanguinarine canadensis*. It is reported to be antimalarial.

Netopilova, M., Drsata, J., Ulrichova, *J. Pharmazie* 51 : 589 - 591.

Stylopine — Alkaloid present in *Corydalis meifolia.*

Bhakuni, D.S., Chaturvedi, R. *J. Nat. Prod.* 1983. 46(3) : 320 - 4.

Tetrahydropalmatine (caseanine) — Alkaloid present in *Corydalis cava* and *Corydalis aurea*. It is reported to be antihypertensive and antioxidant.

Ng, T.B. *et. al., Life Sciences*, Vol. 66(8) : 709 - 723, 2000.

Thaliporphine — Isoquinoline alkaloid present in *Glaucium fimbrilligerum* and *Neolitsea konishii.*

Naunyn Schmiedebergs. *Arch Pharmacol.* 2005. 15.

Su, M.J. *et. al., Eur. J. Pharmacol.* 1994. 11; 254(1-2) : 141 - 50.

Teng, C.M. *et. al., Eur. J. Pharmacol.* 1993. 16, 233(1) : 7-12.

Theabine — Alkaloid present in *Papaver somniferum*. It is reported to be spinal excitant.

Yenhusomidine — Alkaloid present in *Corydalis meifolia.* It is reported to be antispasmodic.

Bhakuni, D.S., Chaturvedi, R. *J. Nat. Prod.* 1983. 46(3) : 320 - 4.

Yenhusomine — Alkaloid present in *Corydalis meifolia.* It is reported to be antispasmodic.

Bhakuni, D.S., Chaturvedi, R. *J. Nat. Prod.* 1983. 46(3) : 320 - 4.

8. FLACOURTIACEAE

Bixin — Carotenoid present in *Bixa indica.*

Chaulmoogric acid — Acid principle present in *Hydnocarpus laurifolia.*

Hydnocarpic acid — Acid principle present in *Hydnocarpus laurifolia.*

Hydnocarpin — Flavonoid present in *Hydnocarpus wightiana*. It is antioxidant.

Reddy, S.V. *et. al.*, *Phytother Res*. 2005. 19(4) : 277 - 81.

Isohydnocarpin — Flavonoid present in *Hydnocarpus wightiana*. It is antioxidant.

Reddy, S.V. *et. al.*, *Phytother Res*. 2005. 19(4) : 277 - 81.

9. CAPPARIDACEAE

Capparine — Alkaloid present in *Capparis decidua*.

Cappariline —Alkaloid present in *Capparis decidua*.

Capparinine — Alkaloid present in *Capparis decidua*.

Cleomine — Glucoside present in *Clemone viscosa*.

Glucocapparin — Glucoside present in *Capparis decidua*.

Viscosin — Glucoside present in *Gynandropsis gyandra*.

10. CRUCIFERAE

Cheiroside - A — Cardiac glycoside present in *Cheiranthus cheiri*. It is reported to be cardiac tonic.

Cheirotoxin — Cardiac glycoside present in *Cheiranthus cheiri*. It is reported to be cardiac tonic. It is less toxic as compared to digitoxin.

Cochlearin (m - hydroxybenzoyl - tropine) — Alkaloid present in *Cochlearia officinalis*.

Erysimoside — Cardiac glycoside present in *Erysimum cheiranthoides* (Brassicaceae). It is reported to be heart tonic.

Lei, Z.H., *et. al.*, *Planta med.* 2001; 67 : 369 - 370.

Espilantol — Active principle present in *Tropaeolum majus*.

Glucoberine — Glycoside present in *Iberis amara*.

Schultz, O.E. and Gmelin, R. *Arch. Pharm. Ber. Dtsch. Pharm. Ges*. 1954; 287(7) : 404 - 11.

Glucoerosin — Glucosinolate prèsent in *Eruca sativa* and *Pringlea antiscorbutica*. It is reported to be antioxidant.

Barillari, J., *et. al.*, *J. Agric. Food Chem.* 2005. 6; 53(7) : 2475 - 82.

lucoerysimoside — Cardiac glycoside present in *Cheiranthus heiri*. It is reported to be cardiac tonic.

lucotropaeolin — Alkaloid present in *Lepidium sativum*.

bamarine — Bitter principle present in *Iberis amara*.

Schultz, O.E. and Gmelin, R. *Arch. Pharm. Ber. Dtsch. Pharm. Ges.* 1954; 287(7) : 404 - 11.

ndole - 3 - Carbinol — Indole-3-carbinol or I3C is a breakdown roduct present in the glucosinolate glucobrassicin, which is present n *Brassica nigra* and *Brassica oleraceäe*. It is reported to be anti-therogenic, anticancer, antioxidant, anti-viral and estrogenic effects.

Albert-Puleo, M. *J. Ethnopharm.* 1983; 9 : 261 - 272.

Bradlow, H.L., Sepkovic, D.W., Telang, N.T., Osborne, M.P. *Ann. NY. Acad. Sci.* 1999; 889 : 204 - 213.

Cover, C.M., Hsieh, S.J., Cram, E.J., *et. al. Cancer Res.* 1999; 59 : 1244 - 1251.

sorhamnetin — Flavonoid present in *Sisybrium irio*.

epidin — Bitter principle present in *Lepidium iberis*.

Myrosin — Glucosinolate present in *Brassica campestris*.

Sinablin — Glucosinolate present in *Brassica campestris*.

Sinapine — Glucosinolate present in *Brassica campestris*.

Sulforaphane — Isothiocyanate present in *Brassica nigra* and *Brassica oleraceae*. It is reported to be anticancer and antioxidant.

Fahey, J.W., Talalay, P. *Food Chem. Toxicol.* 1999; 37 : 973 - 979.

James, D. *et. ȧl.*, *Cancer Epidemiology Biomarkers and Prevention*, Vol. 10, 949 - 954, September 2001.

Nestle, M. *Nutr Rev.* 1998. 56(4 Pt 1) : 127 - 30.

11. FUMARIACEAE

1 - benzylisoquinoline — Isoquinoline alkaloid present in *Fumaria densiflora*.

Allumine — Isoquinoline alkaloid present in *Fumaria densiflora.*

Cancentrine — Isoquinoline alkaloid present in *Dicentra canadensis*

Densiflorine — Isoquinoline alkaloid present in *Fumaria densiflor*

Fumaflorine — Isoquinoline alkaloid present in *Fumaria densiflor*

Fumaricine — Isoquinoline alkaloid present in *Fumaria densiflora*

Fumariline — Isoquinoline alkaloid present in *Fumaria densiflora*

Fumaritine — Isoquinoline alkaloid present in *Fumaria densiflora*

Fumaritridine — Isoquinoline alkaloid present in *Fumar densiflora.*

Fumarine — Isoquinoline alkaloid present in *Fumaria densiflora*

Fumarophycine — Isoquinoline alkaloid present in *Fumar densiflora.*

Parfumine — Isoquinoline alkaloid present in *Fumaria densiflor* It is reported to be hepatoprotective.

Pentatriacontane — Alkaloid present in *Fumaria vaillantii.*

Sinactine — Isoquinoline alkaloid present in *Fumaria densiflora.*

12. POLYGALACEAE

Senegin — Saponin present in *Polygala senega.*

Polygalic acid — Acid principle present in *Polygala senega.*

13. SAPINDACEAE

Adenosine — Anxiolytic principle present in *Euphoria longana.*

Okuyema, E., *et. al.*, *Planta Medica*, Vol. 65(2) : 115 - 119, 1949.

Cleomiscosin - A — Ligno-coumarin present in *Dodonea viscosa.*

Fraxetin — Coumarin present in *Dodonea viscosa.*

Guaranine — Bitter principle present in *Paullinia sorbilis.*

Hautriwaic acid — Diterpenoid present in *Dodonea viscosa.*

ıkorrosside — Saponin present in *Sapindus trifoliatus.*

14. CLUSIACEAE

ımbogin — Isopreylated benzophene derivative present in *rcinia indica.*

ımboginal — Isopreylated benzophene derivative present in *rcinia indica.*

ırcinol — Polyisoprenylated benzophenone present in *Garcinia lica.* It is reported to be anticancer.

ɔgarcinol — Polyisoprenylated benzophenone present in *Garcinia lica.*

ɔrellavone — Flavonoid present in *Garcinia indica.*

ılkensiflavone — Flavonoid present in *Garcinia indica.*

15. HYPERCIACEAE

– epicatechin — Proanthocyandin present in *Hypericum per- atum.*

Kitanov, G. 1983. *Farmatsiya* (Spresent inia) 33: 19-22.

Melzer, R., Fricke, U., Hoelzl, J. *et al., Plant Med* 1988; 54 : 572 - 573.

Melzer, R., Fricke, U. and Holzl, J. (1991). *Arzneimittel - Forschung Drug Research* 41 : 481 - 483.

5 – dihydroxyxanthone — Xanthone present in *Hypericum per- atum, Hypericum roeperanum* and *Hypericum brasiliense.*

Muruganandam, A.V., Ghosal, S. and Battacharya, S.K. (2000). *Biogenic Amines* 15 : 553 - 567.

Rath, G., Potterat, O., Mavi, S. and Hostettmann, K. *Phytochemistry* (1996) 43(2) : 513 - 20.

Rocha, L., *et. al., Phytochemistry* (1994) 36(6) : 1381 - 5.

- hydroxy - 1- methoxyxanthone — Xanthone present in *Hype- um perforatum, Hypericum roeperanum* and *Hypericum brasiliense.*

Muruganandam, A.V., Ghosal, S. and Battacharya, S.K. (200(*Biogenic Amines* 15 : 553 - 567.

Rath, G., Potterat, O., Mavi, S. and Hostettmann, K. In *Phytochemistry* (1996) 43(2) : 513 - 20.

Rocha, L., *et. al.*, *Phytochemistry* (1994) 36(6) : 1381 - 5.

Adhyperforin — Phloroglucinol present in *Hypericum perforatum.*

Maisenbacher, P. and Kovar, K.A. *Planta Medica* 1992; 58 : 29 293.

Ari, Tolonen., Anja, Hohtola. and Jorma, Jalonen. *Phytochemic Analysis.* 2002. Vol. 14, Issue 5, 306 - 309.

Astilbin — Flavonoid present in *Hypericum perforatum.*

Arborine — Alkaloid present in *Glycomis pentaphylla.*

Arborinine — Alkaloid present in *Glycomis pentaphylla.*

Catechin — Proanthocyandin present in *Hypericum perforatum.*

Kitanov, G. 1983. *Farmatsiya* (Spresent inia) 33 : 19 - 22.

Melzer, R., Fricke, U., Hoelzl, J. *et al.*; *Plant Med.* 1988; 5 572 - 573.

Melzer, R., Fricke, U. and Holzl, J. (1991). *Arzneimitt Forschung / Drug Research* 41 : 481 - 483.

Drummondin - D — Phloroglucinol present in *Hypericum dru mondii.*

Jayasuriya, H., Clark, A.M. and McChesney, J.D. In : *J. N Prod.* (1991) 54(5) : 1314 - 20.

Drummondin - E — Phloroglucinol present in *Hypericum dru mondii.*

Jayasuriya, H., Clark, A.M. and McChesney, J.D. In : *J. N Prod.* (1991) 54(5) : 1314 - 20.

Drummondin - F — Phloroglucinol present in *Hypericum dru mondii.*

Jayasuriya, H., Clark, A.M. and McChesney, J.D. In : *J. N Prod.* (1991) 54(5) : 1314 - 20.

Guttiferone - F — Polyisoprenylated benzophenone present in *Allanblackia stuhlmannii.*

Richard, W. *et al., J. Nat. Prod.* 62 : 130 - 132, 1999.

Haronginanthrone — Anthracene derivative present in *Haronga madagascariensis.*

Haronganin — Anthracene derivative present in *Haronga madagascariensis.* It is reported to be hypoglycemic.

Madagascinanthrone — Anthracene derivative present in *Haronga madagascariensis.*

Madagascin — Anthracene derivative present in *Haronga madagascariensis.*

Hydroperoxycariforin — C50-hyrdoxyperoxide present in *Hypericum perforatum.*

Rucker, G., Manns, D., Hartmann, R. *et al.* (1995). *Archive der Pharmazie* 328 : 725 - 730.

Hyperbrasilone — Xanthone present in *Hypericum brasiliense.*

Rocha, L., *et al., Phytochemistry* (1994) 36(6) : 1381 - 5.

Hyperbrasiol - A — Xanthone present in *Hypericum brasiliense.*

Rocha, L. *et al., Phytochemistry* (1995) 40(5) : 1447 - 52.

Hyperforin — Phloroglucinol present in *Hypericum perforatum.*

A. Singer, M. Wonnemann and W.E. Muller. *Pharmacology and Experimental Therapeutics*, Vol. 290, Issue 3, 1363 - 1368, Septemeber 1999.

Adam, P., Arigoni, D., Bacher, A. and Eisnreich, W. *Med. Chem.* 2002. 10; 45 (21) : 4786 - 93.

Biber, A. *et al., Pharmacopsychiatry* 1998; 31 : 36 - 43.

Chatterjee, S.S. *et al., Pharmacopsychiatry* 1998; 31 : 7 - 15.

Cui, Y., *et al., Drug Metab Dispos.* 2004. 32(1) : 28 - 34.

Daniela Tekelova, *et al.*, Thieme : *Planta Medica* - Letters 8 / 2000.

Decosterd, L.A. *et al*; *Planta Med.* 1988; 54 : 560.

Eckert, G.P. and Muller, W.E. *Pharmacopsychiatry* 2001. 34 Suppl. 1 : S22 - 5.

Erdelmeier, C.A.J. *Pharmacopsychiatry* 1998; 31 : 2 - 6.

L. Wolfnder, *et. al., Phytochemical Analysis*. 2003. Volume 14, Issue 8, 290 - 297.

Laakmann, G. *et al., Pharmacopsychiatry* 1998. 31 Suppl. 1 : 54- 9.

Lavinia Cantoni *et. al., Biotransformation and Toxicokinetics*. Society present in Toxicology. 12, 2003.

Luisella Verotta. Dipartimento di Chimica Organica e Industriale, Universita degli Studi di Milano, via Venezian 21, 20133 Milano, Italy.

Muller, W.E., Singer, A. and Wonnemann, M. *Pharmacopsychiatry* 2001. 34 Suppl. 1 : S98 - 102.

Schempp, C.M., *et. al., Br. J. Dermatol.* 2000. 142(5) : 979 - 84.

Watkins, R.E. *et. al., Biochemistry*. 2003. 18; 42(6) : 1430 - 8.

Hypericin — Napthodianthrone present in *Hypericum perforatum*.

Ari Tolonen, Anja Hohtola and Jorma Jalonen. *Phytochemical Analysis*. 2002. Volume 14, Issue 5, 306 - 309.

Bork, P.M., Bacher, S., Schmitz, M.L. *et. al.* (1999). *Planta Medica* 65: 297 - 300.

Couldwell, W.T., Gopalkrishna, R., Hinton, D.R. *et. al.* (1994). *Neurosurgery* 35 : 705 - 710.

Daniela Tekelova, Miroslav Repcak, Erika Zemkova and Jaroslav Toth. Thieme : *Planta Medica*-Letters 8 / 2000.

Duran, N. and Song, P.S.; *Photochem. Photobiol.* 1986; 43 : 677 - 680.

Gulick, R.M., McAuliffe, V., Holden-Wiltse, J. *et. al.* (1999). *Annals present in Internal Medicine* 130 : 510 - 514.

Falk, H. and W. Schmitzberger. 1992. *Monatshefte fur Chemie*. 123 : 731 - 739.

Kerb, R., Brockmoller, J., Staffeldt, B., Ploch, M. and Roots, I. *In : Antimicrob Agents Chemother* (1996) 40(9) : 2087 - 93.

Klose, A. and Wernet, P. In : *Int. Conf AIDS* (1993. 6-11) 9(1) : 470 (abstract No. PO - B26 - 2012).

Kumper, H. Hypericum poisoning in sheep. *In : Tierarztl Prax* (1989) 17(3) : 257 - 61.

Loren, W. Walker. *Portland State University*. 1999.

Mcauliffe, V., *et. al.*, *Natl. Conf. Hum. Retroviruses Relat. Infect.* (1st) (1993. 12 - 16) : 159.

Muldner, H. and Zoller, M. In : *Arzneimittelforschung* (1984) 34(8) : 918 - 20.

Pace, N. and MacKinney, G.; *J. Am. Chemical Soc.* 1941; 63 : 2570 - 2574.

Panossian, A.G., Gabrielian, V., Manvelian, K. *et. al.* (1996). *Phytomedicine* 3 : 19 - 28.

Piovan, A., *et. al.*, *Phytochemistry*. 2004. 65(4) : 411 - 4.

Raffa, R.B. *Life Sciences* 1998; 62 : L265 - L270.

Southwell, I.A. and Campbell, M.H. *Phytochemistry* 1991; 30 : 475 - 478.

Stock, S. and Holz, *J. Planta Med.* 1991; 57 Suppl. 2 : A61 - A62.

Takahashi, I. *et. al.*, *Biochem. Biophys. Res. Commun.* (1989. 29) 165(3) : 1207 - 12.

Thiede, H.M. and Walper, A. In : *J. Geriatr. Psychiatry. Neurol.* (1994) 7 Suppl. 1 : S54 - 6.

Vandenbogaerde, A. de Witte, P. *In : Anticancer Res.* (1995) 15(5A) : 1757 - 8.

Vonsover, A. *et. al.*, *Int. Conf. AIDS* (1996. 7-12) 11(1) : 120 (abstract No. Mo.B. 1377).

Hyperoside (hyperin) — Flavonoid present in *Hypericum perforatum.*

Berghoefer, R. and J. Hoelzl. 1987. *Planta Med.* 53 : 216 - 17.

I - 3 / II – 8 - biapigenin (amentoflavone) — Flavonoid present in *Hypericum perforatum.*

Baureithel, K.H, *et. al.*, *Pharmaceutica Act Helvetiae* 1997; 72 : 153 - 7.

Berghoefer, R. and J. Hoelzl. 1987. *Planta Med.* 53 : 216 - 17.

Berghpresent iner R and Holzl J: *Planta Med.* 1989; 55 : 91.

Isodrummondin – D — Acylphloroglucinol present in *Hypericum perforatum.*

Jayasuriya, H., Clark, A.M. and McChesney, J.D. In : *J. Nat. Prod* (1991) 54(5) : 1314 - 20.

Isoquercetin — Flavonoid present in *Hypericum perforatum.*

Berghoefer, R. and J. Hoelzl. 1987. *Planta Med.* 53: 216-17.

Isouliginosin – B — Flavonoid present in *Hypericum brasiliense.*

Rocha L *et al., Phytochemistry* (1995) 40(5) : 1447 - 52.

Japonicine – A — Flavonoid present in *Hypericum brasiliense.*

Rocha, L., *et. al., Phytochemistry* (1995) 40(5) : 1447 - 52.

Kaempferol — Flavonoid present in *Hypericum perforatum.*

Berghoefer, R. and J. Hoelzl. 1987. *Planta Med.* 53 : 216 - 17.

Leucocyanidin — Proanthocyandin present in *Hypericum perforatum.*

Kitanov, G. 1983. *Farmatsiya,* 33 : 19 - 22.

Melzer, R., Fricke, U., Hoelzl, J. *et al.; Plant Med.* 1988; 54 : 572 - 573.

Melzer, R., Fricke, U. and Holzl, J. (1991). *Arzneimittel-Forschung / Drug Research* 41 : 481 - 483.

Miquelianin — Flavonoid present in *Hypercium perforatum.*

Novoimanine — Phloroglucinol present in *Hypericum perforatum.* It is antibacterial.

Negrash, A.K. *et al., Fitontsidy Mater Soveshch* 1969; 198 - 200.

Patuloside – A — Antibacterial principle present in *Hypericum patulum.*

Ishiguro, K., Yamamoto, R. and Oku, H. *J. Nat. Prod.* 1999. 62(6) : 906 - 8.

Patuloside – B — Antibacterial principle present in *Hypericum patulum.*

Ishiguro, K., Yamamoto, R. and Oku, H. *J. Nat. Prod.* 1999. 62(6) : 906 - 8.

Protohypericin — Napthodianthrone present in *Hypericum perforatum.*

Daniela Tekelova, Miroslav Repcak, Erika Zemkova and Jaroslav Toth. Thieme: *Planta Medica*-Letters 8/2000.

Protopseudohypericin — Napthodianthrone present in *Hypericum perforatum.*

Daniela Tekelova, Miroslav Repcak, Erika Zemkova and Jaroslav Toth. Thieme: *Planta Medica*-Letters 8 / 2000.

Pseudohypericin — Napthodianthrone present in *Hypericum perforatum.*

Ari Tolonen, Anja Hohtola and Jorma Jalonen. *Phytochemical Analysis.* 2002. Volume 14, Issue 5, 306 - 309.

Cameron, D.W. and W.D. Raverty. 1976. *Australian Journal present in Chemistry.* 29 : 1523 - 1533.

Daniela Tekelova, Miroslav Repcak, Erika Zemkova and Jaroslav Toth. Thieme: *Planta Medica*-Letters 8 / 2000.

Kerb, R., Brockmoller, J. Staffeldt, B., Ploch. M. and Roots I. In : *Antimicrob Agents Chemother* (1996) 40(9) : 2087 - 93.

Simmen, U. *et. al., Eur. J. Pharmacol* 2003. 5; 548(3) : 251 - 6.

Takahashi, I., *et. al., Biochem. Biophys. Res. Commun.* (1989) 165(3) : 1207 - 12.

Quercetin — Flavonoid present in *Hypericum perforatum.*

Daniela Tekelova, Miroslav Repcak, Erika Zemkova and Jaroslav Toth. Thieme: *Planta Medica*-Letters 8 / 2000.

Koget, T.A. 1972. *Khim. Prir. Soedin.* (2) : 242 - 3 (CA 77 : 45514b).

Quercitrin — Flavonoid present in *Hypericum perforatum.*

Daniela Tekelova, Miroslav Repcak, Erika Zemkova and Jaroslav Toth. Thieme : *Planta Medica*-Letters 8 / 2000.

Rutaevin — Sesquiterpene present in *Dictamnus dasycarpus* and *Evodia ruracarpa.*

Wang, Z., *et. al., Zhongguo Zhong Yao Za Zhi.* 1992. 17(9) : 551 - 2, 576.

Srivastava, S.D. *et al.*, *Fitoterapia*, 69, 80, 1998.

Rutin — Flavonoid present in *Hypericum perforatum.*

Daniela Tekelova, Miroslav Repcak, Erika Zemkova and Jaroslav Toth. Thieme : *Planta Medica*-Letters 8 / 2000.

Sarothralin - G — Phloroglucinol present in *Hypericum brasiliense.*

Ishiguro K., Yamaki, M., Kashihara, M., Takagi, S. and Isoi, K. In : *Planta Med.* (1990) 56(3) : 274 - 6.

Uliginosin - A — Phloroglucinol present in *Hypericum brasiliense.* It is antibacterial.

Rocha, L., *et. al.*, *Phytochemistry* (1995) 40(5) : 1447 - 52.

16. GUTTIFERAE

Guttiferone - A — Polyisopernylated benzophenone present in *Garcinia livingstonei.* It is anti HIV

Guttiferone - E — Polyisopernylated benzophenone present in *Garcinia livingstonei.* It is anti HIV.

Mangostin — Xanthone present in *Garcinia mangostana.*

Meusone — Phenol present in *Mesua ferrae.*

Mesuol — Lactone present in *Mesua ferrae.*

Morellin — Coloring matter present in *Garcinia morella.* It is anthelmintic.

Xanthochymol — Benzophenone present in *Garcinia xanthochymus.* It is reported to be cytotoxic.

Mutsumoto, K. *et. al.*, *Biol. Pharm. Bull.* 2003. 26(4) : 569 - 71.

17. TILIACEAE

Corchoroside — Cardiac glycoside present in *Cochorus olitorius.*

Soerenby, L. and Lindhale, P.E. *Farmakol Toksikol.* 1964. 27 : 48 - 53.

18. CAMELLIACEAE

Theine — Alkaloid present in *Camellia theifera*. It is central nervous system stimulant

Theophylline — Alkaloid present in *Camellia theifera*. It is bronchodilator and diuretic.

19. MALVACEAE

Asparagin — Base present in *Abutilon indicum, Althoea officinalis* and *Sida cordifolia*.

Bassorin — Mucilage present in *Althoea officinalis*.

Ephedrine — Alkaloid present in *Sida cordifolia*. It is bronchodilator.

Gossypiol — Coloring matter present in *Gossypium herbaceum*.

Gossyptein (8 - hydroxyquercetin) — Flavonoid present in *Hibiscus sabdariffa*.

20. CARYOPHYLLACEAE

Githagoside (Githagin or Agrostemmin) — Saponin present in *Agrostemma githago*.

21. STERCULIACEAE

Adnasonin — Glucoside present in *Adnasonia digitata*.

Caffeine — Alkaloid present in *Sterculia acuminta*. It is central nervous system stimulant.

Gallic acid — Tannin present in *Salmalia malararica*.

Kolanin — Glucoside present in *Sterculia acuminta*.

Mucic acid — Acid principle present in *Sterculia urens*.

Tannic acid — Tannin present in *Salmalia malararica*.

Theobromine — Alkaloid present in *Sterculia acuminta*. It is bronchodilator and diuretic.

22. BYTTNERIACEAE

Theobromine — Alkaloid present in *Theobroma cocoa*. It is bronchodilator and diuretic.

23. TAMARICAEAE

Tamaraxin — Glucoside present in *Tamarix gallica*.

24. ERYTHROXYLACEAE

1 - Hydroxytroptococaine — Tropane alkaloid present in *Erythroxylum novogranatense*

Alpha truxillin — Tropane alkaloid present in *Erythroxylum coca*.

Beta truxillin — Tropane alkaloid present in *Erythroxylum coca*.

Benzoylecogonin — Tropane alkaloid present in *Erythroxylum coca*.

Cocaine — Alkaloid present in *Erythroxylum coca*. It dilates pupil and acts as direct stimulant of the nervous system.

Hygrine — Alkaloid present in *Erythroxylum coca*.

25. CANELLACEAE

6, 7, 10 - trihydroxydaucane — Sesquiterpene present in *Reneilmia cincinnata*. It is reported to be antimalaraial.

Canellal — Sesquiterpene lactone present in *Canella alba*.

26. MELIACEAE

Azadirachtin — Terpene present in *Azadirachta indica*.

Azvaridin — Alkaloid present in *Melia azadarach*.

Bakaynin — Bitter principle present in *Melia azadarach*.

Nimbidin — Terpene present in *Azadirachta indica*.

Margosin — Bitter principle present in *Azadirachta indica*.

Meliantrol — Terpene present in *Azadirachta indica*.

Naregamine — Alkaloid present in *Naregamia alata*.

Nimbidol — Terpene present in *Azadirachta indica*. It is reported to be antitubercular, anti-inflammatory, anti-arthritic and antipyretic.

Nimbiol — Terpene present in *Azadirachta indica*.

Nimbidin — Terpene present in *Azadirachta indica*.

Nimbinin — Terpene present in *Azadirachta indica*.

Nimbin — Terpene present in *Azadirachta indica*.

Nimbinene — Terpene present in *Azadirachta indica*.

Nimbolide — Terpene present in *Azadirachta indica*.

Nimolinone — Terpene present in *Azadirachta indica*.

Odorine — Diamide present in *Aglaia odorata*. It is reported to be anticancer.

Inad, A. *et. al*., *Biol. Pharm. Bull*. 2001. 24(11) : 1282 - 5.

Odorinol — Diamide present in *Aglaia odorata*. It is anticancer.

Inad, A. *et. al*., *Biol. Pharm. Bull*. 2001. 24(11) : 1282 - 5.

Persacine — Alkaloid present in *Melia azadarach*.

Prieurianin — Limonoid present in *Turraea obtusifolia*.

Sarkar, S.D. *et. al*., *Arch Insect Biochem Physiol*. 1997; 35(1-2) : 211 - 7

Rohitukin — Limonoid present in *Turraea obtusifolia* (Meliaceae).

Arch Insect Biochem Physiol. 1997; 35(1-2) : 211 - 7.

Salannum — Terpene present in *Azadirachta indica*. It is reported to be repleent.

27. RUTACEAE

(+) – 8 – methoxyplatydesmine — Furoquinoline alkaloid present in *Evodia merrilli.*

8, 8' '-biskoenigine — Carbazole alkaloid present in *Murraya koengii.*

Wang, Y.S. *et. al. J. Nat. Prod.* 2003. 66(3) : 416 - 8.

Aegelin — Alkaloid present in *Aegle marmelos.*

Aegelinin — Alkaloid present in *Aegle marmelos.*

Barosmin — Bitter principle present in *Barosma betulina.*

β – indoletyhlamike — Alkaloid present in *Evodia rutaecarpa.* It is reported to be central nervous system stimulant, oxytocic and styptic.

Bismurrayafoline — Alkaloid present in *Murraya exotica.*

Candicine — Alkaloid present in *Galipea officinalis.*

Casimiroine — Alkaloid present in *Casimiroa edulis.*

Casimiroedine — Alkaloid present in *Casimiroa edulis.*

Clausine – Z — Carbazole alkaloid present in *Clausena excavata.* It is neuroprotective.

Confusameline (7 – hydroxydictamnine) — Furoquinoline alkaloid present in *Evodia merrillia.*

Dehydroevodiamine — Alkaloid present in *Evodia rutaecarpa.* It is reported to be anticholinesterase, anti-inflammatory, antiarrthymic, oxytocic and nootropic.

Evocarpine — Alkaloid present in *Evodia rutaecarpa.*

Evodiamine — Alkaloid present in *Evodia rutaecarpa.* It is reported to be anti-inflammatory, analgesic and oxytocic.

Evolitrine — Alkaloid present in *Boronia inornata.*

Flindersiamine — Furoquinoline alkaloid present in *Raulinoa echinata.* It is reported to be anti-trypanosominal.

Gamma – fagarine — Furoquinoline alkaloid present in *Ruta graveolens.* It is reported to be mutagenic.

Girinimbine — Carbazole alkaloid present in *Murraya koenigii.*

Graveoline — Alkaloid present in *Ruta graveloens.*

Harmaline — Alkaloid present in *Peganum harmala.*

Harmine — Alkaloid present in *Peganum harmala.*

Heptaphylline — Carbazole alkaloid present in *Clausena harmandiana* and *Citrus reticulata.* It is reported to be antiplasmodial.

Yenjai, C. *et. al., Planta Med.* 2000. 66(3) : 277 - 9.

Heptazolidine — Carbazole alkaloid present in *Clausena harmandiana.*

Chowdhury, B.K., *et. al. J. Chromato,* 1986 : 369, 258.

Heptazoline — Carbazole alkaloid present in *Clausena heptaphylla.*

Hernandonine — Aporphine alkaloid present in *Hernandia nymphaeifolia* (Fabaceae). It is reported to be cytotoxic.

Chen, J.J. *et. al., Planta Med.* 1996. 62(6) : 528 - 33.

Hernangerine — Aporphine alkaloid present in *Hernandia ovigera* and *Hernandia sonora.* It is anti–platelet.

Furkawa, H. and Lu, S.T. *Yakugaku Zasshi.* 1966. 86(12) : 1143-7.

Chen, I.S. *et. al., Planta Med.* 1995. 61(6) : 537 - 9.

Hernovine — Aporphine alkaloid present in *Hernandia nymphaeifolia* (Fabaceae). It is cytotoxic.

Chen, J.J. *et. al., Planta Med.* 1996. 62(6) : 528 - 33.

Heyneanine — Indole alkaloid present in *Ervatamia coronaria.*

Sharma, P. and Cordell, G.A. *J. Nat. Prod.* 1988. 51(3) : 528 - 31.

Heyneatine — Indole alkaloid present in *Ervatamia coronaria.*

Hesperidin — Flavonoid glycoside present in *Citrus aurantium.* It is hemostatic.

Indizoline — Alkaloid present in *Clauesna lanisum.*

Prakash, D. *et al., Indian Journal present in Chemical Society.* B.1980, 19 B, 1075.

Khan, N, *et. al.*, *Phytochemistry*, 1983, 22, 2624.

Yanh, M.H. *et. al.*, *Phytochemistry*, 1988, 27, 445.

Isomahanimbine — Carbazole alkaloid present in *Murraya koenigii.*

Koenigin — Glucoside present in *Murraya koengii.*

Kokusaginine — Furoquinoline alkaloid present in *Dictamnus albus* and *Skimmia laureola.* It is reported to be antidepressant (monoamine oxidase inhibitor).

Maculine — Furoquinoline alkaloid present in *Esenbeckia grandiflora.*

Marmelosin — Furanocoumarin present in *Aegle marmelos.*

Melicarpine — Furoquinoline alkaloid present in *Evodia merrilli.*

Moronic acid — Treiterpene present in *Boronia inornata.*

Mahanimbilol — Carbazole alkaloid present in *Murraya siamensis.*

Mahanimbine — Carbazole alkaloid present in *Murraya koenigii* and *Murraya siamensis.* It is reported to be mosquitocidal, antimicrobial, anti-inflammatory, antioxidant and topoisomrease 1 and 2 inhibitor.

Karina M. Meragelman, *et. al.*, *J. Nat. Prod.* 63 : 427 - 428, 2000.

R.S. Ramsewak, *et.* al., *J. Agric. Food Chem.* Vol. 47, No. 2, p 444 - 447 (1999).

Mahanine — Carbazole alkaloid present in *Murraya koenigii.* It is reported to be mosquitocidal; antimicrobial; anti-inflammatory; antioxidant and topoisomrease 1 and 2 inhibitor.

R.S. Ramsewak, *et. al.*, *J. Agric. Food Chem.* Vol. 47, No. 2, p. 444 - 447 (1999).

Murrayacine — Carbazole alkaloid present in *Murraya koengii.*

Joshi, B.S. *et. al.*, *Tetrahedron*. 1970. 26(6) : 1475 - 82.

Murrayanine — Carbazole alkaloid present in *Murraya koengii.*

Wang, Y.S. *et. al. J. Nat. Prod.* 2003. 66(3) : 416 - 8.

Murrayafoline - A — Carbazole alkaloid present in *Murraya koengii*

Murrayanol — Carbazole alkaloid present in *Murraya koenigii*. It is reported to be mosquitocidal, antimicrobial, anti-inflammatory; antioxidant and topoisomrease 1 and 2 inhibiting activities.

R.S. Ramsewak. *et. al., J. Agric. Food Chem.* Vol. 47, No. 2, p. 444 - 447 (1999).

Murrayin — Glucoside present in *Murraya exotica*.

Naringenin — Flavonoid glycoside present in *Citrus medica*. It is haemostatic.

Noracronycine — Alkaloid present in *Boenninghausenia albiflora* and *Glycomis citrifolia*. It is reported to have anti-platelet effect.

Leu, Y.L. *et al., Phytotherapy Research*. 1998. 12(1) : 77 - 79.

Obacunone — Limonoid present in *Dictamnus albus*. It is reported to be anticancer.

Siamenol — Carbazole alkaloid present in *Murraya siamensis*. It is reported to be anti HIV-.

Karina, M. Meragelman *et. al., J. Nat. Prod.* 63 : 427 - 428, 2000.

Spathulenol — Sesquiterpene present in *Boronia inornata*.

Peganole — Alkaloid present in *Peganum harmala*.

Phlorin — Glycoside present in *Citrus* spp.

Braddock, R.J. and Byran, C.R. *J. Agric. Food Chem.* 2001. 49(12) : 5982 - 8.

Pteleine — Furoquinoline alkaloid present in *Ruta graveolens*. It is reported to be mutagenic.

Ptelefolone — Alkaloid present in *Ptelefolone trifoliata*.

Rutacridone — Acridone alkaloid present in *Ruta graveloens*. It is reported to be mutagenic.

Paulini, H. and Schimmer, O. *Mutagenesis*. 1989. 4(1) : 45 - 50.

Rutaecarpine — Alkaloid present in *Evodia rutaecarpa*. It is reported to be anti-inflammatory.

Rutaevine — Alkaloid present in *Evodia rutaecarpa*. It is reported to be analgesic.

Rutin — Flavonoid glycoside present in *Ruta graveolens*. It i hemostatic.

Shimmianine — Furoquinoline alkaloid present in *Dictamnu albus, Evodia merrilli* and *Xanthoxylum simulams*. It is reported t be cardiac depressant.

Semecarpine — Furoquinoline alkaloid present in *Evodia merrilli*.

Vasicine — Alkaloid present in *Peganum harmala*.

Wuchuyine — Alkaloid present in *Evodia rutaecarpa*.

28. PISOLITHACEAE

Hypaphorine — Indole alkaloid present in *Pisolithus tinctorius*. It i auxin antagonist. It inhibits root hair elongation.

Ditenquo, F.A. *et al*., *Planta Med*. 2000. 211(5) : 722 - 8.

29. CORYNOCARPACEAE

Cibarian — Nitropropanoyl glucoside present in *Corynocarpu laevigatus*.

Corollin — Nitropropanoyl glucoside present in *Corynocarpu laevigatus*.

Corynocarpin — Nitropropanoyl glucoside present in *Corynocarpu laevigatus*.

Coronarian — Nitropropanoyl glucoside present in *Corynocarpu laevigatus*.

30. PITTOSPORACEAE

Pittosporin — Glucoside present in *Pittosporum floribundum*.

31. XANTHOXYLACEAE

Berberine — Alkaloid present in *Xanthoxylum alatum*.

Dictamnine — Alkaloid present in *Xanthoxylum alatum*.

ʼlagnlorine — Alkaloid present in *Xanthoxylum alatum.*

ʼlitidine — Alkaloid present in *Toddalia asiatica.* It is antiviral.

ʼkimmianine — Alkaloid present in *Xanthoxylum alatum.*

ʼanthoplanine — Alkaloid present in *Xanthoxylum alatum.*

32. SIMARUBACEAE

alpha - tigloyloxychaparrinone — Quassinoid present in *Ailan-ʼhus intergrifolia.* It is cytotoxic.

Seida, A.A. *et. al*, In : *Lloydia* (1978) 41(6) : 584 - 7.

ʼilantic acid — Acid principle present in *Ailanthus excelsa.*

ʼlianthone — Quassinoid present in *Ailanthus altissima.* It is ʼhototoxic.

ʼedrine — Alkaloid present in *Simaba cedron.*

ʼhaparrinone — Quassinoid present in *Ailanthus intergrifolia.* It is ʼytotoxic.

Seida, A.A. In : *Diss. Abstr. Int.* (Sci) (1979) 39(10) : 4843.

ʼuassin — Bitter principle present in *Picrasma excelsa*

ʼamaderin — Bitter principle present in *Samadera indica.*

ʼhinjulactone - B — Diterpenoid present in *Ailanthus altissima.*

Furuno, T. *et. al.*, *Chem, Lett.* 1797, 1981.

ʼitexin — Flavonoid present in *Ailanthus excelsa.*

33. ZYGOPHYLLACEAE

ʼuroguaiacidin — Lignan present in *Guaiacum officinale.*

ʼuroguaiacin — Lignan present in *Guaiacum officinale.*

ʼuroguaiaoxidin — Lignan present in *Guaiacum officinale.*

ʼracilin — Spirostanol glycoside present in *Tribulus terrestris.*

ʼuaiacin — Lignan present in *Guaiacum officinale.*

Guaiagutin — Triterpenoid present in *Guaiacum officinale*.

Harmine — Beta carboline alkaloid present in *Tribulus terrestris*.

Harmaline — Beta carboline alkaloid present in *Tribulus terrestris*.

Protodioscin — Steroid saponin present in *Tribulus terrestris*.

34. LINACEAE

Linmarine — Cyanogenic glucoside present in *Linum usitatissimum*.

35. OXALIDACEAE

Potassium oxalate — Present in *Averrhoea carambola*.

36. GERANIACEAE

Gallic acid — Tannin present in *Geranium maculatum*.

Tannic acid — Tannin present in *Geranium maculatum*.

37. CELASTRACEAE

Adouetine — Peptide alkaloid present in *Euonymus atropurpureus*.

Atropupurin — Glucoside present in *Eunoymus atropurpureus*.

Celapanine — Alkaloid present in *Celastrus monosperma*.

Celapanigine — Alkaloid present in *Celastrus monosperma*.

Celastrine — Alkaloid present in *Celastrus paniculatus*.

Celastrol — Nortriterpene present in *Celastrus scandens*. It i reported to be antioxidant, antifungal, anti-inflammatory, cyt protective and neuroprotective.

Anthony, C. Allison. *et al.*, *CNS Drug Reviews*.Vol. 6, No. 1, p 45 - 62.

Evonine — Alkaloid present in *Euonymus atropurpureus* an *Trypterugium hypoglaucum*.

Euonymin — Bitter glycoside present in *Eunoymus atropurpureus*.

Franganin — Peptide alkaloid present in *Euonymus atropurpureus*.

Frangufoline — Peptide alkaloid present in *Euonymus atropurpureus*.

Paniculatine — Alkaloid present in *Celastrus paniculatus*.

Retusine — Alkaloid present in *Mortonia greggii*. It is reported to be anti-inflammatory.

Archinegas, A. *et. al.*, *Z. Naturforsch*. 59c, 237 - 243 (2004).

Scutianine - C — Peptide alkaloid present in *Euonymus atropurpureus*.

Scutianine - D — Peptide alkaloid present in *Euonymus atropurpureus*.

Tingenone — Triterpene present in *Euonymus tingens*. It is reported to be anti-trypanosomal and cytotoxic.

Triptolide — Chemical constituent present in *Tripterygium wilfordii*. It is reported to be anticancer and immunosupressant.

Chen, X. *et al.*, *Blood*. 2005. 1 : 106(7) : 2409 - 16.

M.A. Chan, *et al. Immunopharmacology* 40, 139 (1998) Abstract.

38. RHAMNACEAE

Frangulin — Glucoside present in *Rhamnus frangula*.

Hovenoside — Saponin present in *Hovenia acerba*. It is reported to be sedative.

P. Jain., *et. al.*, *Phytochemistry*, 33, 449, 1993.

Zizyphic acid — Acid principle present in *Zizyphus vulgaris*.

39. ANACADRIACEAE

Anacardic acid — Acid principle present in *Anacardium occidentale* and *Ozoroa insignis*. It is reported to be cytotoxic.

Rea, *et. al.*, *Fitoterpia*. 2003. 74(7- 8) : 732 - 5.

Bhilawanol — Phenol present in *Semecarpus anacardium.*

Cardol — Active constituent present in *Anacardium occidentale.*

Mangiferin — Xanthone present in *Mangifera indica.*

Semecaprol — Phenol present in *Semecarpus anacardium.*

Toxicodendric acid — Acid principle present in *Rhus toxicodendron.*

40. BURSEACAE

3–epi–alpha–amyrin — Triterpene present in *Commiphora molmol.*

Alpha-amyrenone — Triterpene present in *Commiphora molmol.*

Boswellic acid — Pentacyclic triterpene acid present in *Boswellia serrata.* It is reported to be anti-inflammatorry and immunomodulator.

Sharma, M.L., Kaul, A., Khajuria, A., *et. al. Phytotherapy Res.* 1996; 10 : 107 - 112.

Guggulsterone - E — Sterol present in *Commiphora mukul.*

Guggulsterone - Z — Sterol present in *Commiphora mukul.*

Myrrhin — Oleoresin present in *Commiphora myrrha.*

41. FABACEAE

(-) – Glyceoliin — It is present in *Psoralea argophylla.*

Abarnin — Coloring matter present in *Abrus precatorius.*

Abrasine — Alkaloid present in *Abrus precatorius.*

Abricin — Steroidal compound present in *Abrus precatorius.* It is reported to be anti-fertility.

F.Z. Khan, *IAS*, Volume 6, No 2, 1993.

Olsnes, S. and Pihl, A., *FEBS Lett*, 28 : 577 - 580, 1972.

Siddiqui, S., Siddiqui, B.S., Zafar, N., *et. al., ak J. Sci. Ind. Res.*, 21 : 158 - 161, 1978.

Abridin — Steroidal compound present in *Abrus precatorius*. It is reported to be anti-fertility.

F.Z. Khan, Journal present in IAS, Volume 6, No 2, 1993.

Siddiqui, S., Siddiqui, B.S., Zafar, N., *et. al.*, *Pak. J. Sci. Ind. Res.*, 21 : 158 - 161, 1978.

Abrin — Lectin present in *Abrus precatorius*.

Abrine — Alkaloid present in *Abrus precatorius*.

Abrusquinone - A — Isflavanquinone present in *Abrus precatorius*.

Abrusquinone - B — Isflavanquinone present in *Abrus precatorius*.

Abrusquinone - C — Isflavanquinone present in *Abrus precatorius*.

Arburside - E — Triterpene present in *Abrus precatorius*. It is purgative, abortifacient and sweetner.

Aegelinol — Pyranocoumarin present in *Aegle marmelos*.

Alaternin — Anthaquinone present in *Cassia tora*. It is reportd to be antioxidant.

Choi, J.S. *et. al.*, *Arch. Pharm. Res.* 1994. 17(6) : 462 - 6.

Arbalin — Glucoside present in *Abrus precatorius*.

Aurantiobtusin — Anthraquinone present in *Cassia occidentalis*.

Bakuchiol — Phenol present in *Psoralia corylifolia*.

Baptin — Glucoside present in *Baptista tinctoria*.

Baptisin — Glucoside present in *Baptista tinctoria*.

Bonducin — Bitter principle present in *Caesalpinia bonducella*.

Brazilin — Coloring matter present in *Caesalpinia sappan*.

Butin — Polyphenol present in *Butea monosperma*. It is reported to be tyrosine kinase inhibitor.

Butrin — Flavonoid present in *Butea monosperma*. It is reported to be antihepatotoxic.

Wagner, H., *et. al.*, *Planta Med.* 1986. (2) : 77 - 9.

Caesapline — Diterpene present in *Caesalpinia bonducella*.

Cajanone — Flavone present in *Cajanus cajans*. It is reported to be anti HIV.

Castanospermine — Polyhydroxy alkaloid present in *Castanospermum australe*. It is reported to be alpha glucosidase inhibitor and anti HIV.

Cassiaside — Naphthopyrone present in *Cassia tora*. It is reported to be antioxidant.

Choi, J.S. *et al., Arch. Pharm. Res*. 1994. 17(6) : 462 - 6.

Cassidine — Alkaloid present in *Erythrophleum guineense.*

Cassine — Alkaloid present in *Erythrophleum guineense.*

Cassiollin — Anthraquinone present in *Cassia occidentalis.*

Catartine — Alkaloid present in *Coronilla varia.*

Chrysophanic acid — Anthaquinone present in *Cassia acutifolia.*

Chrysobtusin — Anthraquinone present in *Cassia occidentalis.*

Colutequinone — Isoflavonoid present in *Colutea arborescens*. It is reported to be antifungal.

Grovenor, P.W. and Gray, D.O. *Phytochemistry*. 1996. 43(2) : 377-80.

Colutehydroquinone — Isoflavonoid present in *Colutea arborescens*. It is reported to be antifungal.

Grovenor, P.W. and Gray D.O. *Phytochemistry*. 1996. 43(2) : 377-80.

Convicine — Alkaloid present in *Vicia faba*.

Copaivic acid — Resin present in *Copaifera officinalis*.

Corolinine — Alkaloid present in *Coronilla varia.*

Croalbidine — Pyrrolizidine alkaloid present in *Crotalaria albida.*

Croalbinecine — Pyrrolizidine alkaloid present in *Crotalaria albida.*

Croburhine — Pyrrolizidine alkaloid present in *Crotalaria burhia.*

Crotalaburnine — Pyrrolizidine alkaloid present in *Crotalaria verrucosa.*

Crotaverrine — Pyrrolizidine alkaloid present in *Crotalaria verrucosa.*

Daidzein — Ispresent inlavone present in *Glycine max.*

Demethoxykanugin — Alkaloid present in *Pongamia pinnata.*

Chaurasia, S.C. and Jain, P.C. 1978. *Indian J. Hosp. Pharm.* 15(6) : 166 – 168.

Delbergiodin — Flavonoid present in *Dolichos biflorus.*

Dioxifenilalanine — Alkaloid present in *Vicia faba.*

Fraxidin — Coumarin present in *Teramnus labialis.*

Fort D.M. *et. al., Phytochemistry,* Vol. 6(6) : 465 - 467, 1999.

Emodin — Anthaquinone present in *Cassia acutifolia.*

Erthyrophloeine — Glucoside present in *Erythophloeum guinense.*

Erytherine — Alkaloid present in *Erythrina indica.*

Epibaptifolin — Quinolizidine alkaloid present in *Cystisus laburnum.*

Galegine — Gaunidine present in *Galega officinalis.*

Galactene — Hydrocarbon present in *Lupinus albus.*

Gangetin - A — Pterocarpenoid present in *Desmodium gangeticum.*

Ghosh, D. and Anadakumar, A. *Ind. J. Pharmacol,* 1981.

Genistein — Ispresent inlavone present in *Glycine max.*

Glabranine — Flavanone present in *Glychyrrhiza glabra.* It is reported to be antimicrobial and estrogenic.

Kattev, N.S. and Nikonov, G.K. (1972), *Khim. Prir. Soedin,* Vol. 8(6), pp. 805 - 6.

Glabridin — Isoflavone present in *Glychyrrhiza glabra.* It is reported to be antioxidant, antimicrobial and cardioprotective.

Glabrol — Flavonoid present in *Glychyrrhiza glabra.* It is reported to be antimicrobial.

Glycophymine — Alkaloid present in *Glycosmis arborea.*

Lagoja, M.I. *Chemistry and biodiversity*. 2005, Volume 2. Issue 1, Pages 1 - 50.

Glycophymoline — Alkaloid present in *Glycosmis arborea*.

Lagoja, M.I. *Chemistry and biodiversity*. 2005, Volume 2 Issue 1, Pages 1 - 50.

Glycosine — Alkaloid present in *Glycosmis arborea*.

Lagoja, M.I. *Chemistry and biodiversity*. 2005, Volume 2 Issue 1, Pages 1 - 50.

Glycozolidine — Alkaloid present in *Glycosmis arborea*.

Glycozoline — Alkaloid present in *Glycosmis arborea*.

Glycyramarin — Triterpene saponin present in *Glychyrrhiza glabra*.

Glycyrrhizin — Triterpene saponin present in *Glychyrrhiza glabra*. It is reported to be antiviral, anti-inflamamtory and hepatoprotective.

Glycyrrhetic acid — Triterpene saponin present in *Glychyrrhiza glabra*. It is reported to be anti-inflamamtory.

Glyphoside — Falvonoid glycoside present in *Glychyrrhiza glabra*.

Litvineneko, V.I. (1966) *Biol. Abst.* 1967, 48,108638.

Glyzaglabrin — Isoflavone present in *Glychyrrhiza glabra*.

Bhardwaj, D.K. *et. al.*, (1977) *Curr. Sci. Vol.* 46(21), pp. 753.

Glyzarin — Isoflavone present in *Glychyrrhiza glabra*.

Bhardwaj, D.K. *et. al.*, *Phytochemistry,* Vol.16(3), pp. 402 - 403.

Gummic acid — Gum resin present in *Astralagus gummifer*.

Haematoxylin — Crystalline principal present in *Haematoxylon campechianum*.

Helminthosporin — Quinone present in *Cassia occidentalis*.

Homopterocarpin — Flavonoid present in *Pterocarpus santalinus*.

Indican — Glycoside present in *Indigpresent inera tinctoria*.

Indospicine — Pyrrolzolidine alkaloid present in *Indigofera spicata*. It is hepatotoxic.

Indigotin — Coloring matter present in *Indigofera tinctoria.*

Isobutrin — Flavonoid present in *Butea monosperma.* It is reported to be antihepatotoxic. It gets converted into butrin on storage.

Wagner, H. *et. al., Planta Med.* 1986. (2) : 77 - 9.

Isoliquitrin — Chalcone glycoside present in *Glychyrrhiza glabra.*

Isopsoralen — Phenol present in *Psoralia corylifolia.*

Isopteropodine — Alkaloid present in *Uncaria pteropoda.*

Chan, K.C. *et. al., J. Chem. Soc.* 1966; 24 : 2245 - 9.

Isorhamnetin — Flavonoid present in *Cassia acutifolia.*

Kaempferol — Flavonoid present in *Cassia acutifolia.*

Kanugin — Alkaloid present in *Pongamia pinnata.*

Chaurasia, S.C. and Jain, P.C. 1978. *Indian J. Hosp. Pharm.* 15(6) : 166 – 168.

Karanjin — Bitter principle present in *Pongamia pinnata.*

Keivitone — Flavonoid present in *Dolichos biflorus.*

L - dopa — It is found in *Mucuna prurita* and *Vicia faba.*

Licochalcone - A — Isoflavone present in *Glychyrrhiza glabra.*

Licoricidin — Flavonoid present in *Glychyrrhiza uralensis.*

Liquitrin — Chalcone glycoside present in *Glychyrrhiza glabra.*

Lupulidinol — Alkaloid present in *Lupinus albus.*

Luzanine — Alkaloid present in *Lupinus albus.*

Luzinine — Alkaloid present in *Lupinus albus.*

Madurensine — Pyrrozolidine alkaloid present in *Crotolaria agatiflora.* It is reported to be hepatotoxic and pneumotoxic.

Culvenor, C.C. *et al., Chem. Biol. Interact.* 1976. 12(3-4) : 299 - 324.

Medicagol — Coumarin present in *Medicago sativa.* It is reported to be antifungal.

Mimosine — Alkaloid present in *Mimosa pudica.*

Mucronatine — Alkaloid present in *Crotolaria pallida.*

Mucornatinine — Alkaloid present in *Crotolaria pallida.*

Mucuadine — Alkaloid of *Mucuna prurita.*

Mucuadinine — Alkaloid of *Mucuna prurita.*

Mucuadininine — Alkaloid of *Mucuna prurita.*

Mucunadine — Alkaloid of *Mucuna prurita.*

N-methyl cytisine — Quinolizidine alkaloid present in *Baptisia tinctoria.*

Nidgirine — Alkaloid present in *Crotolaria pallida.*

Nilgirine — Pyyrozolidine alkaloid present in *Crotolaria pallida.*

Atal, C.K. and Sawhney, R.S. *Tetrahedron Lett.* 1968. 54 : 5605 - 8.

Obtusifolin — Flavanone glycoside present in *Cassia occidentalis.*

Hansel, R. *et al., Z. Naturforsch B.* 1970. 25(9) : 989 - 94.

Obtusin — Flavanone glycoside present in *Cassia occidentalis.*

Orienntaline — Isoquinoline alkaloid present in *Erythrina verna.*

Palasonin — Sesquiterpene lactone present in *Butea monosperma.* It is reported to be anthelmintic.

Chandra, J.S., Sabir, M. *Indian J. Pharm. Sci.* 40 : 97 - 98 (1978).

Kumar, D. *et. al., Indian J. Pharmacol* 1995; 27 : 161 - 8.

Palastrin — Flavonoid present in *Butea monosperma.*

Paraglastine — Hydrocarbon present in *Lupinus albus.*

Phaseollidin — Flavonoid present in *Dolichos biflorus.*

Physostigmine — Alkaloid present in *Physostigma venenosum.* It is anticholinesterase inhibitor.

Pongamol — Flavonoid present in *Pongamia glabra.*

Precasine — Alkaloid present in *Abrus precatorius.*

Precatorine — Alkaloid present in *Abrus precatorius.*

Pruridine — Alkaloid present in *Mucuna prurita.*

Pruridinine — Alkaloid present in *Mucuna prurita.*

Pruriendine — Alkaloid of *Mucuna prurita.*

Psoralen — Furanocoumarin present in *Psoralea corylifolia.*

Pterocarpin — Flavonoid present in *Pterocarpus santalinus.*

Pteropodine — Alkaloid present in *Uncaria pteropoda.*

Chan, K.C. *et. al., J. Chem Soc.* 1966; 24 : 2245 - 9.

Pterostilbene — Flavonoid present in *Pterocarpus santalinus.*

Pyrocatechin — Tannin present in *Pterocarpus marsupium.*

Rhein — Anthaquinone present in *Cassia acutifolia.*

Rotenoid — Flavonoid present in *Tephrosia purpurea.*

Rubrinusarin — Naphthopyrone present in *Cassia quinquangulata* and *Cassia tora.* It is reported to be antioxidant.

Choi, J.S. *et. al., Arch. Pharm. Res.* 1994. 17(6) : 462 - 6.

Sarothamnoside — Isoflavonoid present in *Cystisus scoparius.*

Scoparin — Glucoside present in *Cystisus scoparius.*

Sennoside - A — Glycoside present in *Cassia acutifolia.*

Sennoside - B — Glycoside present in *Cassia acutifolia.*

S–Methyl - L - cysteine — Alkaloid present in *Capsella bursa pastoris.*

Sparteine — Alkaloid present present in *Cystisus scoparius.*

Stativin — Active principle present in *Lotus corniculatus.*

Tephrosin — Colouring matter present in *Tephrosia purpurea.*

Tragacanthin — Gum resin present in *Astralagus gummifer.*

Trigonelline — Alkaloid present in *Trigonella foneum-graceum.*

Usaramine — Alkaloid present in *Crotolaria pallida.*

Vicenin - 1 — Flavonoid present in *Trigonella foenum-graceum.*

Vicianin — It is present in *Vicia americana.*

Yamogenin (nitogenin) — Steroid sapogenin present in *Trigonella foenum-graceum.*

42. GARRYACEAE

6 - hydroxylspiraqine — Alkaloid present in *Garrya veatchii.*

Garryine — Alkaloid present in *Garrya veatchii.*

Garryfoline — Alkaloid present in *Garrya veatchii.*

Spiraqine — Alkaloid present in *Garrya veatchii.*

Veatchine — Alkaloid present in *Garrya veatchii.*

43. MORINGACAE

Moringine — Alkaloid present in *Moringa olifera.* It is reported to be cardiac stimulant.

Moringinine — Alkaloid present in *Moringa olifera.*

Ptergyospermin — Alkaloid present in *Moringa olifera.* It is reported to be antibiotic.

Spirochine — Alkaloid present in *Moringa olifera.* It is reported to be uterine tonic.

44. ROSACEAE

Agrimophol — Isocoumarin present in *Argimonia pilosa.* It is reported to be anthelmintic.

Amygdalin — Bitter glucoside present in *Prunus pudum.*

Argimonolide — Isocoumarin present in *Argimonia pilosa.* It is reported to be hepatoprotective.

Benedictine — Sesquiterpene present in *Geum elatum.*

Kosidin — Phloroglucinol present in *Hagenia abyssinica.*

Spiredine — Diterpenoid alkaloid present in *Spiraea japonica.*

Li-Ming, F.A.N. *et. al., Journal present in integrative plant biology.* 2005, 47(1): 120 - 123.

Spiradine - A — Diterpenoid alkaloid present in *Spiraea japonica.*

Li-Ming, F.A.N. *et. al., Journal present in integrative plant biology*. 2005, 47(1) : 120 - 123.

Spiradine - B — Diterpenoid alkaloid present in *Spiraea japonica.*

Li-Ming, F.A.N. *et. al., Journal present in integrative plant biology*. 2005, 47(1) : 120 - 123.

Spirasine - V — Diterpenoid alkaloid present in *Spiraea japonica.*

Li-Ming, F.A.N. *et. al., Journal present in integrative plant biology*. 2005, 47(1) : 120 - 123.

Spiraeoside — Flavonoid present in *Filipendula ulmaria.*

Protokosin — Phloroglucinol present in *Hagenia abyssinica.* It is reported to be anti-tumor and toxic.

Woldemariam, T.Z. *et. al., J. Pharm Biomed Anal.* 1992. 10(8) : 555 - 60.

45. PORTULACACEAE

Potassium oxalate — Found in *Portulaca oleracea.*

46. SAXIFRAGACEAE

Dichroin — Glucoside present in *Dichroa ferbrifuga.*

Febrifugine — Alkaloid present in *Dichroa febrifuga.* It is reported to be antimalarial.

Koepfli, J. B. 1947. *J. Am. Chem. Soc.* 69 : 1837.

Koepfli, J. B., J. A. Brockman, Jr., and J. Mat. 1950. *J. Am. Chem. Soc.* 72 : 3323.

Haluginone — Alkaloid present in *Dichroa febrifuga.* It is reported to be inhibitor present in angiogenesis and collagen synthesis.

Elkin, M. *et al., The FASEB Journal.* 2000; 14 : 2477 - 2485.

Granot, I. *et. al.*, (1993) *Biochem. Biophys. Acta.* 1156, 107 - 112.

Nyska, M., A. *et al.*, 1996. *Connect. Tissue Res.* 34 : 97 - 103.

Isofebrifugine — Alkaloid present in *Dichroa febrifuga*. It is reported to be antimalarial.

Koepfli, J. B., J. A. Brockman, Jr., and J. Mat. 1950. *J. Am. Chem. Soc.* 72 : 3323.

47. COMBRETACEAE

7 – hydroxy – 3', 4' - (methylenedioxy) flavone — Flavone present in *Terminalia belerica*. It is anti HIV, antimalarial and antifungal.

Anolignan – B — Lignan present in *Terminalia belerica*. It is anti HIV, antimalarial and antifungal.

Arjunetin — Glucoside present in *Terminalia arjuna*.

Arjunic acid — Triterpene present in *Terminalia arjuna*.

Arjunolone — Flavone present in *Terminalia arjuna*.

Sharma, P.N. *et al., Ind. J. Chem.* 21B : 263, 1982.

Bellericanin — Glucoside present in *Terminalia belerica*. It is cardiac stimulant.

Chebulagic acid — Tannin present in *Terminalia chebula*.

Chebulinic acid — Tannin present in *Terminalia chebula*.

Combretin – A — Alkaloid present in *Combretum micranthum*.

Ellagic acid — Tannin present in *Terminalia arjuna*. It is reported to be antimutagenic.

Kaur, S., Grover, I.S., Kumar, S. *Indian J. Exp Biol.* 1997. 35(5) : 478 - 82.

Fridelin — Glucoside present in *Terminalia arjuna*.

Rhamnocitrin — Flavonoid glycoside present in *Combretum erythrophyllum*. It is reported to be antibacterial and antioxidant.

Martini, N.D. *et. al., Journal of Ethnopharmacology*. Vol. 93, No. 2, pages 207 - 212 (2004).

Rhamnazin — Flavonoid glycoside present in *Combretum erythrophyllum*. It is reported to be antibacterial, anti-inflammatory and antioxidant.

Martini, N.D. *et. al.*, *Journal of Ethnopharmacology*. Vol. 93, No. 2, pages 207 - 212 (2004).

Termilignan — Lignan present in *Terminalia belerica*. It is anti HIV, antimalarial and antifungal.

Terminoside - A — Triterpene glycoside present in *Terminalia arjuna*.

Ali, A. *et al.*, *J. Asian Nat. Prod. Res.* 2003. 5(2) : 137 - 42.

Thannilignan — Lignan present in *Terminalia belerica*. It is anti HIV, antimalarial and antifungal.

48. BARRINGTONIACEAE

Barringtonin — Glucoside present in *Barringtonia acutangula*.

49. MYRTACEAE

Caryophyllin — Terpene present in *Eugenia caryophyllata*.

Eucalyptol or cineole — Terpene present in *Eucalyptus globosus*.

Eugenol — Terpene present in *Eugenia caryophyllata*.

Jambulin — Glucoside present in *Eugenia jambolana*.

Myrtucommulone - A — Acylphloroglucinol present in *Myrtus communis*. It is reported to be antibacterial and antioxidant.

Rotstein, A. *et. al.*, *Antimicrob Agents Chemother*. 1974. 6(5) : 539 - 542.

Rosa, A. *et. al.*, *Free Radic. Res.* 2003. 37(9) : 1013 - 9.

Myrtucommulone - B — Acylphloroglucinol present in *Myrtus communis*.

Rotstein, A. *et. al.*, *Antimicrob Agents Chemother*. 1974. 6(5) : 539 - 542.

Semimyrtucommulone — Acylphloroglucinol present in *Myrtus communis*.

Rosa, A. *et. al.*, *Free Radic Res*. 2003. 37(9) : 1013 - 9.

50. LYTHRACEAE

Heimidine — Alkaloid present in *Heimia salicifolia.*

El-Olmet, M.M. *et al. Lloydia.* 1971. 34(4) : 439 - 41.

Heliotridine — Pyrrolizidine alkaloid present in *Heimia salicifolia.*

Heliotrine — Pyrrolizidine alkaloid present in *Heimia salicifolia.* I is carcinogenic and hepatotoxic.

Schoental, R. *Cancer Research*, Vol. 35, Issue 8 : 2020 - 2024.

Heliotropine — Pyrrolizidine alkaloid present in *Heimi arborescens.*

Heliovicine — Pyrrolizidine alkaloid present in *Heimia arborescens.*

Isopelletierine — Alkaloid present in *Punica granatum.*

Lawsone — Coloring matter present in *Lawsonia alba.*

Nesodine — Alkaloid present in *Heimia salcifolia.* It is reported t be anti-inflammatory.

Lema, W.J. *J. Ethnopharmacol.* 1986. 15(2) : 161 - 7.

Pelletierine — Alkaloid present in *Punica granatum.*

51. APIACEAE

Aethusin — Polyyene present in *Aethusa cynapium.* It is related t cicutoxin.

Anethol — Terpene in volatile present in *Pimpinella anisum.*

Angelicin — Furanacoumarin present in *Angelica archangelica.*

Ng, T.B. *et. al., Life Sciences*, Vol. 66(8) : 709 - 723, 2000.

Apiin — Glucoside present in *Apium graveolens.*

Apiol — Terpene in volatile oil present in *Apium graveolens.*

Archangelicin — Furanacoumarin present in *Angelica archangelica*

Asaresinotannol — Resin present in *Ferula foetida.*

Asiaticoside — Triterpene saponin present in *Centella asiatica.*

akuchiol — Phenol present in *Psoralea corylifolia*

Mehta, G., Naik, U.R., Dev, S. *Tetrahedron* 29 : 1119 - 1125 (1973).

Prakasarao, A.S.C., *et. al.*, *Tetrahedron* 29 : 1127 - 1130 (1973).

ergaptan — Furanacoumarin present in *Heracleum candicans.*

arvene — Terpene in volatile oil present in *Carum carvi.*

olumbianetin — Coumarin present in *Heracleum mantegaz-zianum.*

onine — Alkaloid present in *Conium maculatum.*

oreximine — Isoquinoline alkaloid present in *Apium graveolens.*

Hasrat, J. A., *et. al. J. Pharm. Pharmacol.* 1997; 49(11) : 1145 - 1149.

oriandrol — Terpene in volatile oil present in *Coriander sativum.*

uminol — Terpene in volatile oil present in *Cuminum cyminum.*

erulic acid — Caffeic acid derivative present in *Ferula foetida.*

eraclenin — Furanacoumarin present in *Heracleum candicans.*

Y.N.Sharma, A., Zaman and A.R. Kidwai. *Tetrahedron,* 1964, Vol. 20. 87 - 90.

eraclenol — Furanacoumarin present in *Heracleum candicans.*

Y.N. Sharma, R.C. Sharma, A, Zaman and A.R. Kidwai. *Tetrahedron,* 1964, Vol. 20. 87.

ydrocotyline — Alkaloid present in *Centella asiatica.*

sopimpellin — Furanacoumarin present in *Heracleum candicans.*

hellin — Furanacoumarin present in *Heracleum candicans.*

ledecassoside — Triterpene saponin present in *Centella asiatica.*

arcissine — Flavone glycoside present in *Aethusa cynapium.*

inene — Terpene in volatile oil present in *Foeniculum vulgare.*

isnagin — Furocoumarin present in *Ammi visnaga.*

anthotoxin or ammonidin — Furanacoumarin present in *Ammi ajus.*

52. ONAGRACEAE

Gamma linoleic acid — Polyunsaturated acid present in *Oenothera biennis*. It is reported to be anti-inflammatory and hypolipidemic.

53. PAPAYACEAE

Caricine — Glucoside present in *Carica papaya*.

Carpaine — Alkaloid present in *Carica papaya*. It is cardiac tonic.

Carposide — Glucoside present in *Carica papaya*.

Papain — Protein ferment present in *Carica papaya*.

Pseudocarpaine — Alkaloid present in *Carica papaya*.

54. TURNERACEAE

Damianin — Glucoside present in *Turnera microphylla*.

55. CUCURBITACEAE

4 - Hydroxy - 2 - cyclopentenone — Hydrocarbon present in *Tetrapathaea tetranda*. It is reported to be antibacterial and cytotoxic.

Acetovanillone — Hydroquinone present in *Ecballium elaterium*.

Briocinine — Alkaloid present in *Byronia cretica*.

Byronin — Glucoside present in *Byronia alba*.

Colocynthein — Resin present in *Citrulus colocynthis*.

Colocynthin — Bitter glucoside present in *Citrulus colocynthis*.

Cucurbitine — Alkaloid present in *Beninncasa hisida*.

Deidaclin — Cyanoglucosides present in *Tetrapathaea tetranda*.

Elaterin — Glucoside present in *Citrulus colocynthis* and *Ecballium elaterium*.

Epitetraphyllin - B — Cyanoglucosides present in *Tetrapathaea tetranda*.

Momordicine — Alkaloid present in *Momordica charntia.*

Tetraphyllin - A — Cyanoglucosides present in *Tetrapathaea tetranda.*

Tetraphyllin - B — Cyanoglucosides present in *Tetrapathaea tetranda.*

56. DATISACEAE

Datiscin — Glucoside present in *Datisca cannabina.*

57. ARALIACEAE

Daucosterol — Sterol present in *Oplopanax horridum.*

Eleutherane - A — Polysaccharide present in *Eleuthrococcus senticosus.*

Eleutherane - B — Polysaccharide present in *Eleuthrococcus senticosus.*

Eleutherane - C — Polysaccharide present in *Eleuthrococcus senticosus.*

Eleutherane - D — Polysaccharide present in *Eleuthrococcus senticosus*

Eleutherane - G — Polysaccharide present in *Eleuthrococcus senticosus.*

Eleutheroside - I — Triterpene saponin present in *Eleuthrococcus senticosus.*

Eleutheroside - K — Triterpene saponin present in *Eleuthrococcus senticosus*

Eleutheroside - L — Triterpene saponin present in *Eleuthrococcus senticosus.*

Eleutheroside - M — Triterpene saponin present in *Eleuthrococcus senticosus.*

Isaxidin — Hydroxycoumarin present in *Eleuthrococcus senticosus.* It is reported to be anti-inflammatory.

Panaxadiol — Saponin (ginsenosides) present in *Panax quiquifolium.*

Panaxatriol — Saponin (ginsenosides) present in *Panax quiquifolium*.

Syringin — Glucoside present in *Oplopanax horridum*.

58. CORNACEAE

Cornin — Iridoid monoterpene present in *Cornus florida*. It is reported to be antimitotic.

Nisida, I., Murakami, T.H. *Acta. Med. Okayama*. 1965. 19(1): 1-9.

59. ALANGIACEAE

Alangine — Alkaloid *present in Alangium lamarkii*.

Isotubulosine — Alkaloid present in *Alangium bussyanum*.

Tubulosine — Alkaloid present in *Alangium bussyanum*.

60. CAPRIFOLIACEAE

Vibrunin — Alkaloid *present in Vibrunum foetidium*.

61. ELAEOCARPACEAE

Aristoteline — Alkaloid present in *Aristotelia serrata*.

Aristotelinone — Alkaloid present in *Aristotelia serrata*.

Elaeocarpidine — Alkaloid present in *Elaeocarpus floribundum*.

Serratoline — Alkaloid present in *Aristotelia serrata*.

Serratolenone — Alkaloid present in *Aristotelia serrata*.

62. PODOCAPACEAE

Conidendrin — Lignan present in *Prumnopitys taxifolia*.

Nagilactone - C — Ecdysteroid present in *Podocarpus totara*. It is reported to be cytotoxic and insecticidal.

Podospicatin — Isflavone present in *Prumnopitys taxifolia*: It is reported to have estrogenic effect.

63. MYRTACEAE

Bullatenone — Ketone present in *Lophomyrtus bullata*.

Leptospermone — Ketone present in *Leptospermum scoparium*.

64. MYOPORACEAE

Ngaione — Furanosesquiterpenoid present in *Myoporum laetum*. It is reported to be hepatotoxic.

65. CORIARIACEAE

Coriamyrtin — Alkaloid present in *Coriaria myrtifolia*. It is reported to be analeptic.

Coriarin — Alkaloid present in *Coriaria japonica*.

Tutin — Alkaloid present in *Coriaria arborea*. It is reported to be analeptic and GABA antagonist.

66. MONIMIACEAE

(+) - laurolitsine — Alkaloid present in *Laurelia novae-zelandiae*.

(-) - mecambroline — Alkaloid present in *Laurelia novae-zelandiae*.

(+) - stepharine — Alkaloid present in *Laurelia novae-zelandiae*.

Laureline — Alkaloid present in *Laurelia novae-zelandiae*.

Laurepukine — Alkaloid present in *Laurelia novae-zelandiae*.

Obovanine — Alkaloid present in *Laurelia novae-zelandiae*.

Oxoputerine — Alkaloid present in *Laurelia novae-zelandiae*.

67. RUBIACEAE

10 - Deoxyadifoline — Alkaloid present in *Adina cordifolia*.

10 - Deoxycordifoline — Alkaloid present in *Adina cordifolia*.

Adinin — Coloring matter present in *Adina cordifolia*.

Alizarin — Coloring matter present in *Rubia cordifolia.*

Alpha pederine — Alkaloid present in *Paderia foetida.*

Aricine — Alkaloid present in *Cinchona officinalis.*

Beta - pederine — Alkaloid present in *Paderia foetida.*

Borreriagenin — Iridoid glucoside present in *Borreira verticillata.*

Vieira, J.C.I. *et. al.*, *Org. Lett.,* 1 (8) : 1169 - 1171, (1999.)

Caffeine — Alkaloid present in *Coffea arabica.*

Calycanthine — Pyrrolidinoindoline alkaloid present in *Psychotria malayana.*

Chimonantine — Pyrrolidinoindoline alkaloid present in *Psychotria malayana.*

Cinchonidine — Alkaloid present in *Cinchona officinalis.*

Cinchonine — Alkaloid present in *Cinchona officinalis.*

Cincofulvic acid — Acid principle present in *Cinchona officinalis.*

Daphylloside — Iridoid glucoside present in *Galium humifusum.*

Mitova, M. *et. al.*, *Z.Naturpresent inorsch.* 54c, 488 - 491.

Deoxytubulosine — Alkaloid present in *Alangium bussyanum.*

Feretoside — Iridoid glycoside present in *Gardenia jasminoides.*

Gardenin — Resin present in *Gardenia gummifera.*

Gardenoside — Iridoid glycoside present in *Gardenia jasminoides.*

Gardoside — Iridoid glycoside present in *Gardenia jasminoides.*

Geniposide — Iridoid glycoside present in *Gardenia jasminoides.* It is reported to be anti-tumor and hepatotoxic.

C.J. Wang, *et al.*; *Cancer Lett.* 60, 95 (1991) Abstract.

M.J. Lee, *et al.*; *Anticancer Res.* 15, 411 (1995) Abstract.

Hodgkinsine — Pyrrolidinoindoline alkaloid present in *Psychotria malayana.*

Jaboridine — Alkaloid present in *Pilocarpus jaborandi.*

Jaborine — Alkaloid present in *Pilocarpus jaborandi.*

Manjistin — Coloring matter present in *Rubia cordifolia.*

Morindin — Coloring matter present in *Morinda citrifolia.*

Peseudopurpurin — Coloring matter present in *Rubia cordifolia.*

Pilocarpidine — Alkaloid present in *Pilocarpus jaborandi.*

Pilocarpine — Alkaloid present in *Pilocarpus jaborandi.*

Purpurin — Coloring matter present in *Rubia cordifolia.*

Quinamine — Alkaloid present in *Cinchona officinalis.*

Quinic acid — Acid principle present in *Cinchona officinalis.*

Quinidine — Alkaloid present in *Cinchona officinalis.* It is antiarrthymic.

Quinine — Alkaloid present in *Cinchona officinalis.* It is antimalarial.

Rubidianin — Glucoside pesent in *Rubia cordifolia.* It is reported to be antioxidant.

Tripathi, Y.B., Sharma, M., Manickam, M. *Indian J Biochem Biophys* 1997; 34 : 302 - 6.

Scandoside — Iridoid glucoside present in *Galium humifusum.*

Mitova, M., *et. al*, *Z. Naturpresent inorsch.* 54c, 488 - 491.

Tremetone — Toxin present in *Eupatorium rugosum.*

Beier, R.C. *et. al.*, In : *Nat. Toxins* (1993) 1(5) : 286 - 93.

Xanthopupurin — Coloring matter present in *Rubia cordifolia.*

68. VALERIANCEAE

Jatamansin — Sesquiterpene lactone present in *Nardostachys jatamansi.*

Valerianic acid — Sesquiterpene lactone present in *Valeriana officinalis.*

69. CACTACEAE

Anhalamine — Alkaloid present in *Lophophora williamsii.*

Pellotine — Alkaloid present in *Lophophora williamsii.*

Peyonine — Alkaloid present in *Lophophora williamsii.*

Peyophorine — Alkaloid present in *Lophophora williamsii.*

Peyotine — Alkaloid present in *Lophophora williamsii.*

70. ASTERACEAE

11 alpha, 13 – dihydrohelenalin - [2 - (1 - hydroxyethyl) acrylate] — Sesquiterpene lactone present in *Vernoniopsis caudate.*

18 – hydroxy – 13 – epi - manoyl oxide — Norditerpenoid present in *Grindelia scorzonerifolia.*

18 – O – alpha – l - arabinopyranosylmanoyl oxide — Norditerpenoid present in *Grindelia scorzonerifolia.*

1 – methyl – 4 – methoxy – 8 - (beta – D - glucopyranosy loxy) – 2(1H) – quinolinone — Quinoline glyco-alkaloid present in *Echinops gmelinii.*

2 – hydroxyactriin — Lignan present in *Carthamus tinctorius.*

2, 3, 4, 9 – tetrahydro - 1H - pyrido - (3, 4 - b) indole – 3 - carboxylic acid — Acid principle present in *Cichorium intybus.*

2, 3 – dihyrdo – desacetoxy – matricin — Guaianilide sesuiterpene lactone present in *Achillea millefolium.* It is reported to be anti-inflammatory.

Kastner, U., *et. al.*, In : *PM* 59(7) : A669. 1993.

Ochir, G., Budesinsky, M., Motl, O. In : *PH* 30(12) : 4163. 1991.

4 – alpha – hydroxy – 18 - normanoyl oxide — Norditerpenoid present in *Grindelia scorzonerifolia.*

4 – beta – hydroxy – 19 - normanoyl oxide — Norditerpenoid present in *Grindelia scorzonerifolia.*

4 - methoxy - 8 - (beta - D - glucopyranosyloxy) - 2(1H) - quinolinone — Quinoline glyco-alkaloid present in *Echinops gmelinii.*

7 - angeloylretonecin — Pyrrolizidine alkaloid present in *Senecio nemorensis.*

7 - O - b - D - glucopyranosyl - nutanocoumarin — 5-methyl-coumarin present in *Chaptalia nutans.* It is reported to be antibacterial.

8 - alpha - angeloyloxy - 10 - epi - artabasin — Guaianilide sesuiterpene lactone present in *Achillea millefolium.* It is reported to be anti-inflammatory.

Kastner, U. *et. al.*, In : *PM* 59(7) : A669. 1993.

Ochir, G., Budesinsky, M., Motl, O. In : *PH* 30(12) : 4163. 1991.

9 - angeloylhastanecine — Pyrrolizidine alkaloid present in *Senecio aquaticus.*

Absinthin — Sesquiterpene present in *Artemisia absinthium.*

Achiceine — Alkaloid present in *Achillea millefolium.*

Tewari, J.P., Srivastava, M.C. and Bajpai, J.L. *Tradit. Chin. Med.* 1983. 3(3) : 217 - 8.

Achilleine — Alkaloid present in *Achillea millefolium.* It is reported to be antimalarial. Upon boiling with dilute acids, achilleine yields achilletine.

Achillicin — Guaianilide sesquiterpene lactone present in *Achillea millefolium.* It is reported to be anti-inflammatory.

Kastner, U. *et. al.*, In : *PM* 59(7) : A669. 1993.

Ochir, G., Budesinsky, M., Motl, O. In : *PH* 30(12) : 4163. 1991.

Achillin — Sesquiterpene lactone present in *Achillea millefolium.*

Alpha - peroxyachifolside — Guaianilide sesuiterpene lactone present in *Achillea millefolium.* It is reported to be antiinflammatory.

Kastner, U. *et. al.*, In : *PM* 59(7) : A669. 1993.

Ochir, G., Budesinsky, M., Motl, O. In : *PH* 30(12) : 4163. 1991.

Ambrosin — Sesquiterpene present in *Ambrosia·martima.*

Anabsinthine — Sesquiterpene present in *Artemisia absinthium.*

Anonamine — Pyrrolizidine alkaloid present in *Senecio anonymus.*

Anthecotuloide — Sesquiterpene lactone of *Anthemis cotula.*

Arctigenin — Lignan present in *Arctium lappa.* It is reported to be antiHIV and topoisierase inhibitor.

Arenole — Alpha-pyrone present in *Helichrysum arenarium.*

Arnicin — Sesquiterpene lactone present in *Arnica montana.*

Arnidiol — Sesquiterpene present in *Centipeda minima.*

Artabsine — Sesquiterpene present in *Artemisia absinthium.*

Artemisinin — Sesquiterpene lactone present in *Artemisia annua.* It is antimalarial

Argopyrene — Terpene present in the aromatic oil of *Artemisia drancuculus.*

Arteannuin — Sesquiterpene lactone present in *Artemisia annua.*

Artemisifolin — Sesquiterpene lactone present in *Cnicus benedictus.*

Aguerin - A — Sesquiterpene lactone present in *Cynara scolymus.*

Li, XL *et al., Pergamon-Elsevier Science Ltd. Heterocycles,* 65(2) : 287 - 291.

Ayapanin — Neutral principle present in *Eupatorium ayapana.*

Ayapin — Neutral principle present in *Eupatorium ayapana.*

Azelaic acid — Dicarboxylic acid present in *Cichorium intybus.*

Baccharinoids B1, B2, B3 and B7 — Terpenoids present in *Baccharis megapotamica.* They are reported to be anticancer.

Balchanolide — Guaianilide sesquiterpene lactone present in *Achillea millefolium.*

Tewari, J.P., Srivastava, M.C. and Bajpai, J.L. *J. Tradit. Chin. Med.* 1983. 3(3) : 217 - 8.

Bayogenin — Steroid saponin present in *Solidago canadensis.*

Beta - D - glucopyranosyloxy - 3 - hydroxy - 6(E) - tetradecen - 8, 10, 12 - triyne — Alkylamide present in *Bidens pilosa*.

Betaine — Alkaloid present in *Achillea millefolium*.

Bulgarsenine — Pyrrolizidine alkaloid present in *Senecio nemorensis*.

Brevifolin — Sesuiterpene present in *Centipeda minima*.

Calendulin — Bitter principle present in *Calendula officinalis*.

Caprylic acid — Acid principle present in *Arnica montana*.

Carboxyatractyloside — Kaurene glycoside present in *Xanthium sturmarium*.

Carthamidine — Pigment present in *Carthamus tinctorius*.

Carthamin — Pigment present in *Carthamus tinctorius*.

Carthamone — Flavonol present in *Carthamus tinctorius*.

Centcyamine — Alkaloid present in *Centaurea cyanus*.

Centipedic acid — Acid principle present in *Centipeda officinalis*.

Chrysanthelline A and B — Flavonoids present in *Chrysanthellum americanum*.

Chrysoeriol — Flavonoid aglycone present in *Achillea conferta*.

Cichorin — Sesquiterpene lactone present in *Cichorium intybus*.

Cincin — Sesquiterpene lactone present in *Cnicus benedictus*. It is reported to be anti-inflammatory, antibiotic and cytotoxic.

Schneider, G. and Lachner, I. 1987. *Planta Med.* 53 : 247 - 251.

Vanhaelen-Fastre, R., and Vanhaelen, M. 1976. *Planta Med.* 29 (2) : 179 - 189.

Cis - centcyamine — Alkaloid present in *Centaurea cyanus*.

Cis - moschamine — Alkaloid present in *Centaurea cyanus*.

Clivorine — Pyrrolizidine alkaloid present in *Brachyglottis hectori* and *Ligularia hodgsonii*. It is reported to be inducer present in cell apoptosis.

Coronopilin — Sesquiterpene lactone present in *Parthenium hysterphorus*.

Cynaratriol — Sesquiterpene lactone present in *Cynara scolymus*.

Li, XL *et. al.*, *Pergamon-Elsevier Science Ltd. Heterocycles*, 65(2) : 287 - 291.

Cynarin — Sesquiterpene lactone present in *Cynara scylomus*. It is cholagogue, choleretic, and choliokinetic

Cynaropicrin — Sesquiterpene lactone present in *Cynara scolymus* and *Sausurrea lappa*. It is reported to be anti-inflammatory, cytotoxic and immunomodulator.

Cho, J.Y. *et. al.*, *Eur. J. Pharmacol.* 2000. 23; 398(3) : 399 - 407.

Cho, J.Y. *et. al.*, *Biochem Biophys Res. Commun.* 2004. 23; 313(4) : 954 - 61.

Cho, J.Y. *et. al.*, *Eur. J. Pharmacol*, 492(2-3) : 85-94 (2004.)

Cynaustraline — Pyrrolizidine alkaloid present in *Eupatorium cannabinum, Eupatorium japonicum* and *Crotalaria assamica*.

Edgar, J.A. *et. al.*, In : *Am. J. Chin. Med.* (1992) 20(3-4) : 281 - 8.

Damsin — Sesquiterpene present in *Ambrosia martima*.

Darutyne — Glycoside present in *Sigesbeckia orientalis*.

Daucosterol — Sterol present in *Cichorium intybus*.

Dehydrocynaropicrin — Sesquiterpene lactone present in *Cynara scolymus*.

Li, XL *et. al.*, *Pergamon-Elsevier Science Ltd. Heterocycles*, 65(2) : 287 - 291.

Dehydroanacycline — Alkylamide present in *Anacyclus pyrethrum*.

Delphinidin 3, 5 – di - O - (6 – O – malonyl – beta – D - glucoside) — Anthocyanin present in *Cichorium intybus*.

Delphinidin 3, 5 – di – O – beta – D – glucoside — Anthocyanin present in *Cichorium intybus*.

Delphinidin 3 – O – (6 – O – malonyl – beta – D - glucoside)– 5 – O – beta – D – glucoside — Anthocyanin present in *Cichorium intybus*.

Delphinidin 3 – O – beta – D – glucoside – 5 – O - (6 – O – malonyl – beta – D - glucoside) — Anthocyanin present in *Cichorium intybus*.

Doronine — Pyrrolizidine alkaloid present in *Emilia sonchifolia.*

Dulcoside – A — Glycoside present in *Stevia rebudiana.*

Echinacein — Alkylamide present in *Echinacea purpurea.* It has antifeedent activity.

Echinacin — Alkylamide present in *Echinacea purpurea.*

Echinatine — Pyrrolizidine alkaloid present in *Eupatorium cannabinum*

Ecliptasaponin – C — Triterpenoid glucoside present in *Eclipta alba.*

Ecliptasaponin – D — Triterpenoid glucoside present in *Eclipta alba.*

Eclabatin — Triterpenoid glucoside present in *Eclipta alba.*

Upadhyay, R.K., *et. al.*, *J. Asian Nat. Prod. Res.* 2001; 3(3) : 213-7.

Ecliptine — Alkaloid present in *Eclipta alba.*

Elephantopin — Sesquiterpene lactone of *Elephantopus scaber.* It is reported to be anticancer.

Enhydrin — Sesquiterpene present in *Enhydra flucutans.*

Epineoadenostylone — Sesquiterpene lactone present in *Packera candidissima.*

Erucifoline — Pyrrolizidine alkaloid present in *Senecio jacoboea.*

Eufoliatin — Flavonoid present in *Eupatorium littorale.*

Eufoliatorin — Flavonoid present in *Eupatorium littorale.*

Eupafolin — Sesquiterpene lactone present in *Eupatorium perfoliatum* and *Eupatorium littorale.*

Eupakirunsins A-E — Sesquiterpene lactone present in *Eupatorium kiirunense.* It is reported to be cytotoxic.

Eupatolid — Sesquiterpene lactone present in *Eupatorium cannabinum.*

Eupatorin — Sesquiterpene lactone present in *Eupatorium perfoliatum*. It is reported to be cytotoxic.

Eupatoriopicrin — Sesquiterpene lactone present in *Eupatorium cannabinum*. It is reported to be cytotoxic.

Euperfolide — Flavonoid present in *Eupatorium littorale.*

Euperfolitin — Flavonoid present in *Eupatorium littorale.*

Floridanine — Pyrrolizidine alkaloid present in *Senecio aureus.*

Florilenalin — Sesquiterpene lactone present in *Centipeda minima.*

Florosenine — Pyrrolizidine alkaloid present in *Senecio aureus.*

Fuschsisencionine — Pyrrolizidine alkaloid present in *Senecio nemorensis.*

Gaillardin — Sesquiterpene lactone present in *Gaillardia pulchella*. It is reported to be cytotoxic.

Gaudichanolides A and B — Clerodane diterpenoids present in *Baccaharis gaudichaudiana.*

Grindeline — Alkaloid present in *Grindelia robusta.*

Grossheimin — Sesquiterpene lactone present in *Cynara scolymus.* It is reported to be cytotoxic.

Li, XL *et. al.*, *Pergamon-Elsevier Science Ltd. Heterocycles*, 65(2) : 287 - 291.

Hectorine — Pyrrolizidine alkaloid present in *Brachyglottis hectori.*

Helenalin (atlantolactone) — Lactone present in *Helenium autmnale.* It is anticancer.

Helianthol - A — Sesquiterpene alcohol present in *Helianthus tuberosus.*

M. Miyazawa and H. Kameoka. *Phytochemistry*, 20, 1040 - 1042 (1983).

Helianthoside - C — Triterpene saponin present in *Helianthus tuberosus.*

Bader, G., *et. al.*, *Pharmazie*. 1997. 52(11) : 836 - 8.

Ielianthinin — Glycoside present in *Helianthemum canadense.*

Iexametoxyflavone — Flavone present in *Ageratum conyzoides.*

Iispidium — Glycoside present in *Baccharis timera.*

Iispidulin — Glycoside present in *Baccharis timera.*

Iomotaraxsterol — Sterol present in *Taraxacum officinale.*

Iydroxyachillin — Guaianilide sesquiterpene lactone present in *\chillea millefolium.*

Tewari, J.P., Srivastava, M.C. and Bajpai, J.L. *J Tradit. Chin. Med.* 1983. 3(3) : 217 - 8.

ntegerrimine — Pyrrolizidine alkaloid present in *Packera ·andidissima* and *Petasites hybridus.*

ntybin — Sesquiterpene lactone present in *Cichorium intybus.*

sodeoxyelephantopin — Terpenoid present in *Elephantopus ·arolinianus.* It is anticancer.

sosalipurposide — Chalcone glycoside present in *Helichrysum ırenarium.*

sotussilagine — Pyrrolizidine alkaloid present in *Tussilago arfara.*

vain — Bitter principle present in *Achillea moschata.*

acobine — Pyrrolizidine alkaloid present in *Petasites hybridus* and *Senecio cineraria.*

aconine — Pyrrolizidine alkaloid present in *Senecio cineraria.*

acozine — Pyrrolizidine alkaloid present in *Senecio aquaticus.*

hanol — Diterpenoid present in *Grindelia scorzonerifolia.*

actucin — Sesquiterpene lactone present in *Cichorium intybus* and *actuca virosa.*

eicarposide — Phenolic glycoside present in *Solidago* spp.

eucodin — Guaianilide sesquiterpene lactone present in *Achillea nillefolium.*

Tewari, J.P., Srivastava, M.C. and Bajpai, J.L. *J. Tradit. Chin. Med.* 1983 Sep; 3(3) : 217 - 8.

Levulin — Dextrin like substance present in *Taraxacum officinale.*

Ligularidine — Pyrrolizidine alkaloid present in *Emilia coccinea.*

L - strachydrine — Alkaloid present in *Achillea millefolium.*

Tewari, J.P., Srivastava, M.C., Bajpai, J.L., *J. Tradit. Chin. Med.* 1983. 3(3) : 217 - 8.

Lycopsamine — Pyrrolizidine alkaloid present in *Eupatorium cannabinum.*

Malephantin — Germacranolide present in *Elephantopus mollis.*

Matricine — Sesquiterpene present in *Artemisia absinthium.*

Matricarianol — Polyyene present in *Grindelia camporum.*

Matricarianolacetate — Polyyene present in *Grindelia camporum.*

Medusasides A and B — Lignan glucosides present in *Saussurea medusa.*

Mellisic acid — Fatty acid present in *Taraxacum officinale.*

Millifin — Sesquiterpene lactone present in *Achillea millefolium.*

Tewari, J.P., Srivastava, M.C., and Bajpai, J.L. *J. Tradit. Chin. Med.* 1983. 3(3) : 217 - 8.

Millifolide — Sesquiterpene lactone present in *Achillea millefolium.*

Tewari, J.P., Srivastava, M.C., Bajpai, J.L., *J. Tradit. Chin. Med.* 1983. 3(3) : 217 - 8.

Monocrotaline — Pyrrolizidine alkaloid present in *Senecio aureus.* It inhibits Na-K ATPase pumps. It is reported to be inducer of angiogenesis.

Moschamine — Alkaloid present in *Centaurea cyanus.*

Moschatine — Alkaloid present in *Achillea moschata.*

Neoadenostylone — Sesquiterpene lactone present in *Packera candidissima.*

Neohesperidoside — Flavonoid present in *Cirsium japonicum.*

Neoligularidine — Pyrrolizidine alkaloid present in *Emilia coccinea.*

Neopulchellidine — Alkaloid present in *Gaillardia pulchella.*

Yanagita, M. *et. al. Tetrahedron Lett.* 1970. 2 : 131 - 4.

Neosenkirkine — Pyrrolizidine alkaloid present in *Emilia coccinea.*

Nortracheloside — Lignan present in *Cnicus benedictus.*

O - acetylerucifoline — Pyrrolizidine alkaloid present in *Senecio jacoboea.*

Otosenine — Pyrrolizidine alkalod present in *Senecio aureus* and *Senecio lorenthii.*

Oxalic acid — Acid principle present in *Chrysanthemum leucanthemum.*

Parthenolide — Sesquiterpene present in *Tanacetum parthenium.* It is reported to be anti-inflammatory.

Pectolinarin — Flavonoid present in *Cirsium japonicum.* It is reported to be analgesic and anti-inflammatory.

Petasinine — Pyrrolizidine alkaloid present in *Brachyglottis hectori.*

P - hydroxyphenylacetic acid — Fatty acid present in *Taraxacum officinale.*

Phytosterin - B — Sterol present in *Bidens pillosa.*

Sarq, T.M. *et. al., Acta Pharm. Hung.* 1991. 61(6) : 317 - 23.

Platyphyllin — Pyrrolizidine alkaloid present in *Senecio nemorensis.*

Polypodine - B — Flavonoid present in *Leuzea (Rhaptonicum) carthamoides.* It is embyrotoxic.

Kosar, K. *et. al., Pharmazie.* 1997. 52(5) : 406 - 7.

Mamadalieva, N.Z. *et. al., Collection present in Czechoslovak Chemical Communications* Abstracts : 2004, 69(8) 1675 - 1680.

Ponasterone - A — Triterpene present in *Leuzea (Rhaptonicum) carthamoides.*

Ponticaepoxide — Polyyene present in *Achillea millefolium*, *Artemisia annua* and *Echinacea purpurea.*

Pulicanadienals A and B — Sesquiterpene present in *Pulicaria canariensis.*

Pulicanadiene A, B and C — Sesquiterpene present in *Pulicaria canariensis.*

Pulicanadienol — Sesquiterpene present in *Pulicaria canariensis.*

Pulicanarals A, B and C — Sesquiterpene present in *Pulicaria canariensis.*

Pulicanol — Sesquiterpene present in *Pulicaria canariensis.* It is reported to be cytotoxic.

Pulicanone — Sesquiterpene present in *Pulicaria canariensis.*

Pulchellidine — Alkaloid present in *Gaillardia pulchella.*

Yanagita, M., *et. al. Tetrahedron Lett.* 1970. 2 : 131 - 4.

Pulchellin — Alkaloid present in *Gaillardia pulchella.*

Yanagita, M., *et. al. Tetrahedron Lett.* 1970. 2 : 131 - 4.

Pulioplopanones A and B — Sesquiterpene present in *Pulicaria canariensis.*

Pyrethrin — Resin present in *Anacyclus pyrethrum.*

Pyrethrine — Alkaloid present in *Anacyclus pyrethrum.*

Quercetagetin 7 - glucoside — Flavonoid present in *Tagetes coronopifolia.*

Rebaudoside — Glycoside present in *Stevia rebudiana.*

Retrosine — Pyrrolizidine alkaloid present in *Brachyglottis hectori*, *Packera candidissima, Petasites hybridus, Senecio aureus* and *Senecio cineraria.*

Reynosine — Sesquiterpene lactone present in *Tanacetum vulgare.*

Riddelline — Pyrrolizidine alkaloid present in *Senecio aureus.*

Rinderine — Pyrrolizidine alkaloid present in *Eupatorium cannabinum.*

Safflomine - A (hydroxysafflor yellow A) — Pigment present in *Carthamus tinctorius.*

Safflomine - B (safflor yellow B) — Pigment present in *Carthamus tinctorius.*

Salonitenolic — Sesquiterpene lactone present in *Cnicus benedictus* and *Centaurea deusta.* It is reported to be antibacterial and antifungal.

Anastasia, K., *et. al.*, *Z. Naturforsch.* 57c, 75D80 (2002).

Santonin — Sesquiterpene lactone present in *Artemisia cina.*

Sarracin — Pyrrolizidine alkaloid present in *Senecio nemorensis.*

Sausserine — Alkaloid present in *Saussurea lappa.*

Scopoletin — Coumarin present in *Artemisia afra.* It is reported to be antihypertensive.

Guantai, A.N. and Addae-Menash, L.A. *Pharmaceutical Biology*, Vol. 37(5) : 351 - 356, (1999.)

Senecine — Pyrrolizidine alkaloid present in *Senecio cineraria.*

Senecionine — Pyrrolizidine alkaloid present in *Adenostyles alliariae, Brachyglottis hectori, Senecio aureus, Senecio vulgaris, Packera candidissima* and *Petasites hybridus.*

Seneciphylline — Pyrrolizidine alkaloid present in *Adenostyles alliariae, Petasites hybridus, Senecio cineraria* and *Senecio vulgaris.*

Senkirkine — Pyrrolizidine alkaloid present in *Emilia sonchifolia, Packera candidissima, Petasites hybridus, Tussilago farfara* and *Senecio cineraria.*

Sesamine — Lignan present in *Anacyclus pyrethrum.*

Silymarin — Flavanolignan present in *Silybum marianum.*

Spartioidine — Pyrrolizidine alkaloid present in *Adenostyles alliariae.*

Spartioidine — Pyrrolizidine alkaloid present in *Senecio aquaticus.*

Sphaeranthine — Alkaloid present in *Sphaeranthus indicus.*

Spermidine — Pyrrolizidine alkaloid present in *Senecio vulgaris.*

Spilanthol — Sesquiterpene present in *Spilanthes calva.*

Steviol — Aglycone present in *Stevia rebudiana.*

Steviolbioside — Glucoside of *Stevia rebudiana.*

Stevioside — Glucoside of *Stevia rebudiana.*

Supinine — Pyrrolizidine alkaloid present in *Eupatorium cannabinum.*

Tancetin — Sesquiterpene lactone present in *Tanacetum vulgare.*

Taraxecerin — Bitter principle present in *Taraxacum officinale.*

Taraxsterol — Sterol present in *Taraxacum officinale.*

Tomenphantopin A and B — Terpenoids present in *Elephantopus tomentosus.* They are reported to be anticancer.

Tomenphantin - A — Germacranolide present in *Elephantopus tomentosus.*

Tomenphantin - B — Germacranolide present in *Elephantopus tomentosus.*

Trachelogenin — Lignan present in *Cnicus benedictus.* It is reported to be anti HIV.

Schroder, H.C. *et. al., Z. Naturforsch* [C]. 1990. 45(11-12) : 1215 - 21

Paska, C. *et. al., Phytotherapy Research* 12(Supplement 1) : S30 - S32.

Tremetone — Toxin present in *Eupatorium rugosum.*

Beier, R.C. *et. al.*, In : *Nat. Toxins.* (1993)1(5) : 286 - 93.

Tribonelline — Alkaloid present in *Achillea millefolium.*

Trideca - 5 - ene - 7, 9, 11 - triyne - 3 - ol — Polyyene present in *Arctium lappa* and *Bidens tripartite.*

Trimethylamine — Alkaloid present in *Arnica montana.*

Tussilagine — Pyrrolizidine alkaloid present in *Tussilago farfara.*

Usaramine — Pyrrolizidine alkaloid present in *Packera candidissima.*

Vernadalol — Sesquiterpene lactone present in *Vernonia cineria.* It is reported to be anti-psoriatic.

Veronine — Alkaloid present in *Vernonia anthelmintica.*

Virgaureoside - A — Phenolic glycoside present in *Solidago* spp.

Vulgarin — Sesquiterpene lactone present in *Artemisia vulgaris.* It is reported to be hypoglycemic and anti-tumor.

Wedeleolactone — Lactone present in *Eclipta alba.*

Agarwal, A., Venkataraman, B.V. *Phytother Res.* 2003. 17(4) : 420 - 1.

Xanthosturmarin — Glucoside present in *Xanthium strurmarium.*

71. LOBELIACEAE

Inflatine — Alkaloid present in *Lobelia inflata.*

Isolobinine — Alkaloid present in *Lobelia inflata.*

Lobeline — Alkaloid present in *Lobelia inflata.* It is narcotic.

Lobelanine — Alkaloid present in *Lobelia inflata.*

Lobelanidine — Alkaloid present in *Lobelia inflata.*

Norlobealnine — Alkaloid present in *Lobelia inflata.*

72. CAMPANULACEAE

Fagomine — Alkaloid present in *Adenophora triphylla.* It is reported to be hypoglycemic.

73. ERICACEAE

Arbutin — Glucoside present in *Arctostaphylos Uva Ursi.* It is diuretic.

Ericolin — Bitter glucoside present in *Arctostaphylos Uva Ursi.*

Methylarbutin — Bitter glucoside present in *Arctostaphylos Uva Ursi.*

Methyl salicylate — Counter-irritant principle present in *Gaultheria procumbens.*

Gaultherialine - A — Alkaloid present in *Gaultheria nummularioides.*

Gaultherin — Bitter glucoside present in *Gaultheria procumbens.*

74. PRIMULACEAE

Anagalline — Saponin present in *Anagallis arvensis.*

Cyclamin — Saponin present in *Cyclamen persicum.*

75. PLUMBAGINACEAE

Plumbagin — Napthoquinone present in *Plumbago rosea* and *Plumbago zeylenica.* It is antitumor.

Uma Devi, *Pharmaceutical Biology* 1999, Vol. 37, No. 3, 231-236.

76. EUCMMIACEAE

Geniposidic acid — Iridoid glycoside present in *Eucommia ulmoides.*

Li y *et. al., Biological* and *Pharmaceutical Bulletin.* 1998. 21(12) : 1306 - 10.

77. APOCYNACEAE

Y - akummicine — Alkaloid present in *Alstonia scholaris.*

(+) - akuammidine — Alkaloid present in *Voacanga grandifolia.*

(+) - quebrachamine — Alkaloid present in *Vinca minor.*

1, 2 - dehydroaspidospermidine — Alkaloid present in *Vinca minor.*

2 - deoxyvobtusine — Alkaloid present in *Voacanga grandifolia.*

3 - Epiconamine — Alkaloid present in *Holarrhonea antidysenterica.*

10 - methoxyaffinisine — Alkaloid present in *Alstonia macrophylla.*

10 - methoxycathafoline — Alkaloid present in *Alstonia macrophylla.*

10 - methoxy - deacetylakuammiline — Alkaloid present in *Vinca minor.*

11 - methoxy - eburnamonine — Alkaloid present in *Vinca minor.*

11 - methoxyvincamine — Alkaloid present in *Vinca minor.*

14 - epivincamine — Alkaloid present in *Vinca minor.*

16 - acetylstrospeside — Cardioactive glycoside present in *Adenium obesum* (Apocynaceae). It is reported to be cytotoxic.

Hafman, J.J. and Cole, J.R. *J. Pharm. Sci.* 1977. 66(9) : 1336 - 8.

16 - methoxy - 20 - oxo - 1 - vincadifformine — Alkaloid present in *Vinca minor.*

16 - methoxyminovincinine — Alkaloid present in *Vinca minor.*

18 - oxovobtusine — Alkaloid present in *Voacanga grandifolia.*

19S - heyneanine — Alkaloid present in *Tabernaemontana laeta.*

Walter, L.B., *et al., J. Braz. Chem. Soc.* Vol. 12, No. 3.

19, 20 - epoxyconoduramine — Bisindole alkaloid present in *Tabernaemontana johnstonii*. It is reported to be anticancer.

Kingston, D.G. *et. al., J. Pharm. Sci.* 1978. 67(2) : 249 - 51.

20 - hydroxyvincamine — Alkaloid present in *Vinca minor.*

Ajamaline — Alkaloid of *Rauvolfia serpentina.*

Ajamlicine — Alkaloid of *Rauvolfia serpentina.*

Akuammigine — Alkaloid present in *Alstonia scholaris.*

Akuammidine — Alkaloid present in *Alstonia scholaris.*

Allamandicin — Iridoid glucoside present in *Allamanda blanchettii.* It is reported to be anti HIV.

Allamandin — Iridoid glucoside present in *Plumeria lancifolia.*

Alstophylline — Alkaloid present in *Alstonia macrophylla.*

Alstonine — Alkaloid present in *Alstonia macrophylla.*

Alstovenine — Alkaloid present in *Alstonia ventata*. It is reported to be antifungal.

Amataine — Alkaloid present in *Voacanga grandifolia.*

Aricine — Alkaloid present in *Rauvolfia vomitoria.*

Benzoylvincamajine — Alkaloid present in *Alstonia macrophylla.*

Boonein — Lactone present in *Alstonia boonei.*

Carapanaubine — Alkaloid present in *Rauvolfia vomitoria.*

Cathafoline — Alkaloid present in *Alstonia macrophylla.*

Concuressine — Alkaloid present in *Holarrhonea antidysenterica.*

Conamine — Alkaloid present in *Holarrhonea antidysenterica.*

Conkurchine — Alkaloid present in *Holarrhonea antidysenterica.*

Conessidine — Alkaloid present in *Holarrhonea antidysenterica.*

Conessimine — Alkaloid present in *Holarrhonea antidysenterica.*

Conimine — Alkaloid present in *Holarrhonea antidysenterica.*

Connesine — Alkaloid present in *Holarrhonea antidysenterica.*

Conodurine — Alkaloid present in *Tabernaemontana laeta.*

Walter, L.B. *et al., J. Braz. Chem. Soc.* Vol. 12 No. 3.

Coronaridine — Alkaloid present in *Tabernaemontana laeta.*

Walter, L.B. *et al., J. Braz. Chem. Soc.* Vol. 12 No. 3.

Corymine — Alkaloid present in *Hunteria zeylanica*. It is reported to be anti-inflammatory.

Reanmongkol, W. *et al., Biol. Pharm. Bull.* 1995. 18(1) : 33 - 6.

Corsaymine — Alkaloid present in *Hunteria zeylanica.*

Ditamine — Alkaloid of *Alstonia scholaris.*

Dimethoxyalstonine — Alkaloid present in *Alstonia macrophylla.*

Dimethoxyeburnamonine — Alkaloid present in *Vinca minor.*

Dysobinin — Tetranotriterpenoid present in *Dysophylla binectariferum.* It is reported to be anti-inflammatory and central nervous system depressant.

Echitamidine — Alkaloid present in *Alstonia venenata.*

Echitamine — Alkaloid of *Alstonia scholaris.*

Echitanine — Alkaloid of *Alstonia scholaris.*

Echitovenaldine — Alkaloid present in *Alstonia venenata.*

Echitovenidine — Alkaloid present in *Alstonia venenata.*

Eburnamenine — Alkaloid present in *Vinca minor.*

Eburnamine — Alkaloid present in *Vinca minor.*

Eburnamonine — Alkaloid present in *Vinca minor.*

Epiheteroconessine — Alkaloid present in *Holarrhonea antidysenterica.*

Epivincamine — Alkaloid present in *Vinca minor.*

Fruticosine — Indole alkaloid present in *Kopsia fruticosa.*

Fruticosamine — Indole alkaloid present in *Kopsia fruticosa.*

Funtumafrine - C — Alkaloid present in *Chonemorpha macrophylla.* It is reported to be muscle relaxant.

Kumar, Ray. and Das. *Indian Journal present in Pharmacology.* 2005 (37) 2 : 116 - 19.

Gabunamine — Bisindole alkaloid present in *Tabernaemontana johnstonii.* It is reported to be anticancer.

Kingston, D.G. *et. al., J. Pharm. Sci.* 1978. 67(2) : 249 - 51.

Holacetine — Alkaloid present in *Holarrhonea antidysenterica.*

Holadysamine — Alkaloid present in *Holarrhonea antidysenterica.*

Holadysine — Alkaloid present in *Holarrhonea antidysenterica.*

Holarrhenine — Alkaloid present in *Holarrhonea antidysenterica.*

Holarrhidine — Alkaloid present in *Holarrhonea antidysenterica.*

Holarrhimine — Alkaloid present in *Holarrhonea antidysenterica.*

Holarrhidine — Alkaloid present in *Holarrhonea antidysenterica.*

Holarrhimine — Alkaloid present in *Holarrhonea antidysenterica.*

Holarrhine — Alkaloid present in *Holarrhonea antidysenterica.*

Holonamine — Alkaloid present in *Holarrhonea antidysenterica.*

Williaman, *et. al.*, *Lloydia*, 33 S, 1, 1970.

Hongheloside - A — Cardioactive glycoside present in *Adenium obesum* (Apocynaceae). It is reported to be cytotoxic.

Hpresent, infman. J.J. and Cole, J.R. *J. Pharm. Sci.* 1977. 66(9) : 1336 - 8.

Honghelin — Cardioactive glycoside present in *Adenium obesum* (Apocynaceae). It is reported to be cytotoxic.

Hpresent infman J.J. and Cole, J.R. *J. Pharm. Sci.* 1977. 66(9) : 1336 - 8.

Isoburnamine — Alkaloid present in *Vinca minor.*

Isovincamine — Alkaloid present in *Vinca minor.*

Isoandwicene — Alkaloid present in *Rauvolfia vomitoria.*

Japindine — Dimeric steroidal alklaloid present in *Chonemophora macrophylla.*

Kopsine — Indole alkaloid present in *Alstonia venenata.*

Kopsinine — Indole alkaloid present in *Alstonia venenata.* It is hepatoprotective.

Huang, W.Y. and Liu, G.T. *Zhongguo Yao Li Xue Bao.* 1989. 10(5) : 461 - 4.

Kurchessine — Alkaloid present in *Holarrhonea antidysenterica.*

Kurchaline — Alkaloid present in *Holarrhnoea antidysentrica.*

Kurchamine — Alkaloid present in *Holarrhonea antidysenterica.*

Kurchine — Alkaloid present in *Holarrhonea antidysenterica.*

Kurchiphylline — Alkaloid present in *Holarrhnoea antidysentrica.*

Kurchiphyllamine — Alkaloid present in *Holarrhnoea antidysentrica.*

Leurocolombine — Alkaloid present in *Vinca rosea.*

Tafur, S. *et. al., J. Pharm. Sci.* 1975. 64(12) : 1953 - 7.

Lochnerine — Alkaloid present in *Alstonia macrophylla.*

Locherninine — Indole akaloid present in *Vinca rosea.* It is reported to be cytotoxic.

Tin-Wa M., *et. al. J. Pharm. Sci.* 1968. 57(12) : 2167 - 9.

Macalstonidine — Alkaloid present in *Alstonia macrophylla.*

Macralstonine — Alkaloid present in *Alstonia macrophylla.*

Macrocarpamine — Alkaloid present in *Alstonia macrophylla.*

Friedrich, Mayer., Manfred, Hesse., *Helvetica Chimica Acta.* Vol. 61, Issue.1, 337 - 351.

Macrophylline — Alkaloid present in *Alstonia macrophylla.*

Methoxyminovincine — Alkaloid present in *Vinca minor.*

Minorine — Alkaloid present in *Vinca minor.*

Minovinceine — Alkaloid present in *Vinca minor.*

Minovincine — Alkaloid present in *Vinca minor.*

Minovincinine — Indole alkaloid present in *Vinca rosea.*

Laflamme, P. *et. al., Plant Physiol*, 2001, Vol. 125, 189 - 198.

Minovine — Alkaloid present in *Vinca minor.*

Mitoridine — Alkaloid present in *Rauvolfia vomitoria.*

Nareline — Indole alkaloid present in *Alstonia scholaris.*

Morita, Y. *et. al., Helv Chim Acta.* 1977 1; 60(4) : 1419 - 32.

Neriodin — Cardiac glycoside of *Nerium odorum.*

Neriodorein — Cardiac glycoside of *Nerium odorum.*

Neriodorin — Cardicac glycoside of *Nerium odorum*.

N_b - methylvoachalotine — Alkaloid present in *Tabernaemontana laeta* (Apocynaceae).

Walter, L.B. *et al., J. Braz. Chem. Soc.* Vol. 12 No. 3.

Norconessine — Alkaloid present in *Holarrhonea antidysenterica*.

Perakine — Alkaloid present in *Rauvolfia vomitoria*.

Pericalline — Indole alkaloid present in *Catharanthus trichophyllus*. It is reported to be anticancer.

Segelman, A.B. and Farnsworth, N.R. *J. Pharm. Sci.* 1974. 63(9): 1419 - 22.

Perivincine — Alkkaloid present in *Vinca minor*.

Picrinine — Alkaloid present in *Alstonia scholaris*.

Morita, Y. *et. al., Acta Hel Chim.* 60, 1419, 1977.

Rastogi, R.C. *et. al., Experimentia*, 26, 1056, 1970.

Raugalline — Alkaloid present in *Rauvolfia vomitoria*.

Raumitorine — Alkaloid present in *Rauvolfia vomitoria*.

Raunitidine — Alkaloid present in *Rauvolfia vomitoria*.

Rauvanine — Alkaloid present in *Rauvolfia vomitoria*.

Rauvomiline — Alkaloid present in *Rauvolfia vomitoria*.

Rauvomitine — Alkaloid present in *Rauvolfia vomitoria*.

Rauvoxine — Alkaloid present in *Rauvolfia vomitoria*.

Rauvoxidine — Alkaloid present in *Rauvolfia vomitoria*.

Renoxidine — Alkaloid present in *Rauvolfia vomitoria*.

Rescidine — Alkaloid present in *Rauvolfia vomitoria*.

Reserpiline — Alkaloid present in *Rauvolfia vomitoria*.

Reserpoxidine — Alkaloid present in *Rauvolfia vomitoria*.

Rhazine — Alkaloid present in *Alstonia scholaris* and *Rhazya stricta*.

Gupta, R.S. *et. al., Asian J. Androl* 2002. 4 : 175 - 178.

Al-Doghairi, M.A. *et. al., Journal present in Herbs, Spices* and *Medicinal Plants.* 2002. 10(2).

Tabernamine — Alkaloid present in *Tabernaemontana lueta* and *Tabernaemontana johnstonii.* It is reported to be anticancer.

Kingston, D.G. *et. al., J. Pharm. Sci.* 1978. 67(2) : 249 - 51.

Walter, L.B. *et al., J. Braz. Chem. Soc.* Vol. 12 No. 3.

Tabersonine — Alkaloid present in *Voacanga grandifolia.*

Reserpine — Alkaloid present in *Rauvolfia serpentina.* It is antihypertensive.

Tubotaiwine — Alkaloid present in *Alstonia scholaris.*

Sarpagine — Alkaloid present in *Rauvolfia vomitoria.*

Scholarine — Alkaloid present in *Alstonia scholaris.*

Banerji, J., *et al., Indian J. Chem.* 23B, 5, 455, 1984.

Banerji, J., *et al., Phytochemistry.* 20, 540, 1981.

Keawpradub, N., *et. al., Phytochemistry.* 37, 1745, 1994.

Serpenctine — Alkaloid present in *Rauvolfia vomitoria.*

Seredine — Alkaloid present in *Rauvolfia vomitoria.*

Serdamine — Alkaloid present in *Rauvolfia vomitoria.*

Somalin — Cardioactive glycoside present in *Adenium obesum* (Apocynaceae). It is reported to be cytotoxic.

Hofman, J.J. and Cole, J.R. *J. Pharm. Sci.* 1977. 66(9) : 1336 - 8.

Thevetine — Cardiac glycoside of *Thevetia nerifolia.*

Strictamine — Alkaloid present in *Alstonia scholaris.*

Bhattachraya, S.K. *et. al., Indian J. Exp. Biol.* 1979. 17(6) : 598 - 600.

Tombozine — Alkaloid present in *Diplorrhyncus mossambicensis.*

Quevauviller. A. and Takenaka, Y. *J. Physiol.* (Paris). 1962. 54 : 403 - 4.

Villastonine — Alkaloid present in *Alstonia macrophylla.*

Vimifoline — Alkaloid present in *Rauvolfia vomitoria.*

Vincadifformin — Alkaloid present in *Vinca minor.*

Vincarubine — Alkaloid present in *Vinca minor.* It is reported to be cytotoxic.

Proksa, B., D. Uhrin, *et. al.*, (1988). *Planta Medica* 54(3) : 214 - 218.

Vincadine — Alkaloid present in *Vinca minor.*

Vincamedine — Alkaloid present in *Vinca minor.*

Vincamidine — Alkaloid present in *Vinca minor.*

Vincamine — Alkaloid present in *Vinca minor.*

Vincaminine — Alkaloid present in *Vinca minor.*

Vincaminoreine — Alkaloid present in *Vinca minor.*

Vincaminoridine — Alkaloid present in *Vinca minor.*

Vincaminorine — Alkaloid present in *Vinca minor.*

Vincanorine — Alkaloid present in *Vinca minor.*

Vincareine — Alkaloid present in *Vinca minor.*

Vincarorine — Alkaloid present in *Vinca minor.*

Vincatine — Alkaloid present in *Vinca minor.*

Vincesine — Alkaloid present in *Vinca minor.*

Vincine — Alkaloid present in *Vinca minor.*

Vincinine — Alkaloid present in *Vinca minor.*

Vincoridine — Alkaloid present in *Vinca minor.*

Vincorine — Alkaloid present in *Vinca minor.*

Vincoside — Alkaloid present in *Vinca minor.*

Vincristine — Alkaloid present in *Vinca minor.*

Vinine — Alkaloid present in *Vinca minor.*

'inomine — Alkaloid present in *Vinca minor*.

'inoxine — Alkaloid present in *Vinca minor*.

Bosch, J., M. L. Bennasar, *et. al*. (1987). *Anales De Quimica Serie C Quimica Organica Y Bioquimica* 83(1) : 66 - 69.

'intsine — Alkaloid present in *Vinca minor*.

'oacamine — Alkaloid present in *Tabernaemontana laeta*.

Walter, L.B. *et al., J. Braz. Chem. Soc*. Vol. 12, No. 3.

'oacangine — Alkaloid present in *Tabernaemontana laeta*. It is eported to be anasthetic and anti-fertility.

Walter, L.B. *et al., J. Braz. Chem. Soc*. Vol. 12 No. 3.

'oachalotine — Alkaloid present in *Tabernaemontana fuschiae-olia*.

'obtusine — Alkaloid present in *Voacanga grandifolia*.

'omalidene — Alkaloid present in *Rauvolfia vomitoria*.

'omilenine — Alkaloid present in *Rauvolfia vomitoria*.

78. ASCLEPIADACEAE

Asclepiadin — Glucoside present in *Asclepias curassavica*.

Calotoxin — Glucoside present in *Calotropis procera*.

Calotropin — Glucoside present in *Calotropis procera*. It is reported o be anticancer.

Ceropegin — Alkaloid present in *Ceropegia acuminta*.

Condurangin — Glucoside present in *Condurango gonolobus*. It is eported to be anticancer.

Desgiucouzarin — Cardiac glycoside present in *Asclepias syriaca*.

Doemine — Alkaloid present in *Doemia extensa*.

Dregein — Alkaloid present in *Dregea volubilis*.

Gurmarin — Peptide present in *Gymnema sylvestre*.

Gymnamine — Alkaloid present in *Gymnema sylvestre.*

Gymnemic acid — Triterpene glucoside present in *Gymnema sylvestre.* It is reported to be anti-sweet and hypoglycemic.

Frugoside — Steroid glycoside present in *Calotropis procera.*

P - methoxy salicylic aldehyde — Coumarin present in *Hemidesmus indicus.*

Rhodexin - A — Cardiac glycoside present in *Cryptostegia grandiflora.* It is cytotoxic.

Mitsuhashi, M. *et. al., Chem. Pharm. Bull.* 19, 282, 1971.

Journal Pharm Sci., 1972, 61, 570.

Syriogenin — Cardiac glycoside present in *Asclepias syriaca.*

Syriobioside — Cardiac glycoside present in *Asclepias syriaca.*

Tylophornidine — Alkaloid present in *Tylophora indica.* It is antileukemic.

Tylophorine — Alkaloid present in *Tylophora indica.* It is reported to be anti-asthmatic and bronchodilator.

Tylophornine — Alkaloid present in *Tylophora indica.*

Uscharidin — Cardiac glycoside present in *Calotropis procera.*

Uscharin — Cardiac glycoside present in *Calotropis procera.*

Xysmalogenin — Cardiac glycoside present in *Asclepias syriaca.*

79. LOGANIACEAE

12 - hydroxystrychnine — Indole alkaloid present in *Strychnos ignatii.*

15 - hydroxystrychnine — Indole alkaloid present in *Strychnos nux-vomica.*

Angustine — Indole alkaloid present in *Strychnos angustiflora.*

Alpha colubrine — Indole alkaloid present in *Strychnos nux-vomica*

Beta colubrine — Indole alkaloid present in *Strychnos nux-vomica.*

Brucine — Alkaloid present in *Strychnos nux-vomica*. It is reported to be local anesthetic.

Gelsemine — Alkaloid present in *Gelsemium sempervirens*.

Gelseminine — Alkaloid present in *Gelsemium sempervirens*.

Gelsidine — Indole alkaloid present in *Gelsemium sempervirens*.

Gelsevirine — Indole alkaloid present in *Gelsemium sempervirens*.

Icajine — Alkaloid present in *Strychnos nux-vomica*.

Loganin — Glucoside present in *Strychnos nux-vomica*.

Sempervirine — Indole alkaloid present in *Gelsemium sempervirens*.

Strychnine — Alkaloid present in *Strychnos nux-vomica*. It is convulsant.

80. GENTIANACEAE

Amarogentin — Bitter glucoside present in *Swertia chirata*. It is reported to be antileshminial.

Ray, S., Majumdar, H.K., Chakarvarty, A.K., *et. al. J. Nat. Prod.* 1996; 59 : 27 - 9.

Chiratanin — Xanthone present in *Swertia chirata*.

Chiratenol — Bitter principle present in *Swertia chirata*.

Chiratol — Xanthone present in *Swertia chirata*.

Eniclavine — Triterpenoid alkaloid present in *Swertia chirata*.

Episwertinol — Bitter principle present in *Swertia chirata*.

Gentialutine — Alkaloid present in *Gentiana lutea*.

Gentianic acid — Acid principle present in *Gentiana lutea*.

Gentianidine — Alkaloid present in *Gentiana olivieri*.

Mansoor, A. *Pak. J. Bot.*, 32(1) : 105 - 109, 2000. Abstract.

Gentianine — Alkaloid present in *Gentiana lutea* and *Gentiana olivieri*. It is reported to be anxiolytic.

Bhattacharya, S.K., *et. al.*, *Pharm. Sci.* 1974. 63(8) : 1341 - 2.

Mansoor, A., *Pak. J. Bot.*, 32(1) : 105 - 109, 2000. Abstract.

Gentiobetine — Alkaloid present in *Gentiana lutea.*

Gentiocrucine — Alkaloid present in *Swertia chirata.*

Gentimarine — Alkaloid present in *Gentiana lutea.*

Gentiopicrin — Bitter glucoside present in *Swertia chirata.*

Mangiferin — Xanthone present in *Swertia chirata.* It is reporetd to be hypoglycemic.

Oliverine — Alkaloid present in *Gentiana olivieri.* It is reported to be antihypertensive.

Quevauviller, A. and Hamonniere, M.C.R. *Acad. Sci. Hebd. Seances. Acad. Sci. D.* 1977. 3; 284(1) : 93 - 6.

Nieto, M. *et al.*, *Lloydia.* 1976. 39(5) : 350 - 6.

Oliveridine — Alkaloid present in *Gentiana olivieri.* It is reported to be antihypertensive and cytotoxic.

Quevauviller, A. and Hamonniere, M.C.R. *Acad. Sci. Hebd. Seances Acad. Sci. D.* 1977. 3; 284(1) : 93 - 6.

Nieto, M. *et. al*, *Lloydia.* 1976. 39(5) : 350 - 6.

Stevigny, *et. al.*, *Cur. Med. Chem. Anti Cancer agents*, 2005, 5, 173 - 182.

Oliveramine — Alkaloid present in *Gentiana olivieri.*

Oliveroline — Alkaloid present in *Gentiana olivieri.* It is reported to be antiparkisnson.

Quevauviller, A. and Hamonniere, M.C.R. *Acad. Sci. Hebd. Seances Acad. Sci. D.* 1977. 3; 284(1) : 93 - 6.

Swerchinin — Xanthone present in *Swertia chirata.* It is reported to be hypoglycemic.

Swertanone — Bitter principle present in *Swertia chirata.*

Xanthone present in *Swertia chirata.*

Swertenol — Bitter principle present in *Swertia chirata.*

Swertinin — Xanthone present in *Swertia chirata.*

Swertimarine — Bitter glucoside present in *Enicostemma littorale.*

81. CONVOLVULACEAE

Betaine — Alkaloid present in *Evolvulus alsinoides.*

Chanoclavine — Minor alkaloid present in *Ipomoea tricolor.*

Schultes, R.E. *Journal present in Psychedlic Drugs* Vol. 9 (No.3) 1977.

Elymoclavine — Alkaloid present in *Ipomoea nil.*

Evolvine — Alkaloid present in *Evolvulus alsinoides.*

M. N. Guruswami, *et. al.*, Procedings Indian Acdemy Sciences, Section A, Vol. 8 : 119 - 120.

Ipalbidine — Indolizidine alkaloid present in *Ipomoea alba.* It is reported to be non-narcotic analgesic.

Wang, L.M. and Chu, Y.H. *Yao Xue Xue Bao.* 1996. 31(11) : 806 - 11.

Zhou, J. *et. al., Zhongguo Yao Li Xue Bao.* 1988. 9(2) : 107 - 11.

Ipalbine — Indolizidine alkaloid present in *Ipomoea alba.*

Jalapin — Glucoside present in *Ipomoea purga.*

Phytosterolin — Sterol present in *Ipomoea fistulosa.*

Gupta, O.C. *et. al., Planta Med.* 1971. 20(2) : 172 - 7.

Turpethine — Glucoside present in *Ipomoea turpetheum.*

82. BORAGINACEAE

Alkanin — Napthoquinone present in *Alkanna tinctoria* and *Arnebia euchroma.* It is reported to be antifungal (active against *Candida albicans*).

Chien-Chang Shen., *et. al., J. Nat. Prod.*, 65(12), 1857 - 1862, 2002.

Coromandaline — Alkaloid present in *Heliotropium currassavum.*

Curassavine — Alkaloid present in *Heliotropium currassavum.*

Cynaustine — Alkaloid present in *Cynoglossum lanceolatum.*

Cynaustraline — Alkaloid present in *Cynoglossum lanceolatum.*

Heleurine — Pyrrozolidine alkaloid present in *Helitropium europaeum.*

Heliocoromandaline — Alkaloid present in *Heliotropium currassavum.*

Helifoline — Pyrrolizidine alkaloid present in *Heliotropium ovlifolium.*

Mohanraj, S. *et. al.*, *Phytochemistry*, 1981, 20(80) : 1991.

Heliscabine — Pyrrolizidine alkaloid present in *Heliotropium scabrum.*

Lakshmanan, A.J., Shanmugasundaram, S., *Phytochemistry*, 1995, 39(2) : 473.

Heliovicine — Alkaloid present in *Heliotropium currassavum.*

Heliotropin — Alkaloid present in *Heliotropium indicum.*

Longitubine — Pyrrolizidine alkaloid present in *Hackelia longituba.*

Roitman, J.N., *Aust. J. Chem*, 1988, 41, 1827.

Neolatifoline — Pyrrolizidine alkaloid present in *Hackelia longituba.*

Roitman, J.N. Longitubine, neolatifoline, new pyrrolizidine alkaloids from *Hackelia longituba* [J]. *Aust. J. Chem.*, 1988, 41, 1827.

Retronecine — Pyrrozolidine alkaloid present in *Heliotrpoium indicum.* It is hepatotoxic.

Mattalocks, A.R. *Toxicol Lett.* 1982. 14(1-2) : 111 - 6.

83. ETHRETIACEAE

Ehretinine — Pyrrolizidine alkaloid present in *Ehretia aspera.*

Suri, O.P., Jamwal, R.S., Suri, K.A., *et al. Phytochemistry*, 1980, 19 : 1273.

84. MYRSINACEAE

Christembine — Alkaloid present in *Embelia ribes.*

Embelin — Resin present in *Embelia ribes.* It is reported to be anthelmintic.

Gupta, O.P., *et. al., Indian J. Phy. Trans. of Med. and Phys. Soc of Calcutta*, VII 1., 85.

Rapanone — Benzoquinone present in *Ardisia colorata* (Myrsinaceae) and *Rourea santiloids.* It is reported to be anthelmintic, anti-inflammatory and anti-spermoatogenic.

Calle, J. *et. al., Journal of Ethnopharmacology.* Vol. 71, No. 3, 521 - 525 (2000).

Krishnamurthy, V., *et. al., Current Sci.* Vol. 34, 16 - 17.

Murthy, K.V., *et. al. Tetraherdon.* 21, 1445, 1965.

Ogawa, H., *et. al., Chem. Pharm. Bull*, 16, 1709, 1968.

Ospina, L.F., *et. al., Planta Med.* 2001. 67(9) : 791 - 5.

Ramaih, C.H.E., *et. al., JICI*, Vol. XLVIII (11), 196. 1976.

85. STYRACAEAE

Benzoic acid — Acid principle present in *Styrax benzoin.*

Cinnamic acid — Acid principle present in *Styrax benzoin.*

86. SYMPLOCOACEAE

Colloturine — Alkaloid present in *Symplocos racemosa.*

Loturine — Alkaloid present in *Symplocos racemosa.*

Loturidine — Alkaloid present in *Symplocos racemosa.*

87. OLEACEAE

Olecanthol — Active principle present in *Olea europea.*

Oleoeuropin — Active constituent present in *Olea europea.* It is antioxidant.

88. JASMINACEAE

Arbortristoside – A — Glucoside present in *Nyctanthes arbortristis*. It is reported to be antiallergic.

Arbortristoside – C — Glucoside present in *Nyctanthes arbortristis*.

Jasminine — Alkaloid present in *Jasminum grandiflorum*.

Nyctanthine — Alkaloid present in *Nyctanthes arbortristis*. It is reported to be antiallergic.

Salicylic acid — Acid principle present in *Jasminum grandiflorum*.

89. SOLANACEAE

5,20 α – (R) – dihdroxy - 6 α, 7 α - epoxyl - 1- oxo - (5 α) – witha-2,24 - dienolide Withaferin – A — Withanolide present in *Withania somnifera*. It is immnumodulator.

Bahr, V. and Hansel, R., *Planta Medica*. (1962). Vol. 44(1), 32-33.

Anaferine — Alkaloid present in *Withania somnifera*.

Rother, A., *et. al.*, *Chem. Ind.*, (1962) No. 14, 654 - 655.

Anahygrine — Alkaloid present in *Withania somnifera*.

Leary, J.D. *et. al.*, *Chem. Abstr.*, 1964, 60, 107 - 836 g.

Anisodamine — Alkaloid present in *Anisodus tanguticus*. It is anticholinergic.

Anisodine — Alkaloid present in *Anisodus tanguticus*. It is anticholinergic.

Atropine — Alkaloid present in *Atropa belladonna*.

Brunfelsamide — Convulsant principle present in *Brunfelsia grandiflora*.

Capsaicin — Oleoresin present in *Capsicum annum*.

Capsanthin — Carotenoid present in *Capsicum annum*.

Capsicin — Alkaloid present in *Capsicum annum*.

Cucsohygrine — Alkaloid present in *Withania somnifera*.

Daturalactone (hyoscyamilactol) — Withanolide present in *Hyoscyamus niger.*

Cui, Y.M., *et. al., J. Nat. Prod.,* 62 (10), 1445 - 1447, 1999.

Duboisine — Alkaloid present in *Duboisia myoporoides.*

Dulcamrin — Glucoside present in *Solanum dulcamra.*

Hopeanine — Alkaloid present in *Brunfelsia uniflora.* It is reported to be anti-inflammatory.

Hygrine — Alkaloid present in *Withania somnifera.*

Hyoscine — Alkaloid present in *Hyoscyamus niger.*

Hyoscyamine — Alkaloid present in *Hyoscyamus niger.*

Isopelletriene — Alkaloid present in *Withania somnifera.*

Littorine — Alkaloid of *Hyoscyamus muticus.*

Lycopene — Carotenoid present in *Lycopersicum escultentum.*

Manaceine — Alkaloid present in *Brufelsia uniflorus.* It is reported to be lymphatic system stimulant.

Plowman, Harvard University, Botanical Museum Leaflets, Vol. 25 No. 10, 1977, p. 289.

Manacine — Alkaloid present in *Brufelsia uniflorus.* It is reported to be lymphatic system stimulant.

Plowman, Harvard University, Botanical Museum Leaflets, Vol. 25 No. 10, 1977, p. 289.

Mandragorine — Alkaloid present in *Mandagora officinarum.*

Meteolodine — Alkaloid present in *Datura stramonium.*

Nicotine — Alkaloid present in *Nicotiana tabacum.*

Physalin — Bitter glucoside present in *Physalis minima.*

Pseudopelletriene — Alkaloid present in *Withania somnifera.*

Physolactone - B — Withanolide present in *Physalis peruviana.*

Ray, A.B., *et. al., Chem.* and *Ind.* 17 : 62.

Scopolamine — Alkaloid present in *Scopola carniolica.*

Soladulcamarine — Alkaloid present in *Solanum dulcamra.*

Soladulcidine — Alkaloid present in *Solanum dulcamra.*

Solamargenine — Alkaloid present in *Solanum dulcamra.*

Solanidine — Alakloid present in *Solanum indicum.*

Solanocarpine — Alakloid present in *Solanum xanthocarpum.*

Solanocarpidine — Alakloid present in *Solanum xanthocarpum.*

Solasonine — Alkaloid present in *Solanum nigrum.*

Tigloidine — Alkaloid present in *Datura stramonium.*

Torvogenin — Steroid saponin present in *Solanum torvum.*

Tropine — Alkaloid present in *Withania somnifera.*

Visamine — Alkaloid present in *Withania somnifera.*

Truntneva, E.A. (1971). *Chem. Abstr.*, 1973, 79, 273 – 152.

Withaferin - A — Withanolide present in *Withania somnifera.* It is anticancer.

Ali, M., M. Shuaib, *et al., Phytochemistry* (1997) 44(6) : 1163 - 1168.

Choudhary, K. and Neogy, R.K. *Biochem. Pharmacol.* (1975), Vol. 24(8), 919 - 920.; *Biol. Abstr.* 1975, 60, 62270.

Devi, P.U., Akagi, K., Ostapenko, V., Tanaka, Y., Sugahara, T., Withaferin- *Int. J. Radiat. Biol.* 1996. 69(2) : 193 - 7.

Devi, P.U. *Indian J. Exp. Biol.* 1996; 34 : 927 - 932.

Fuska, J., B. Proska, J.S. Williamson and J. Rosazza. *Folia Microbiol.* (Prague), 1987, 32 : 112 - 115.

Gupta, A.P., R.K. Verma, *et. al. Journal of Medicinal and Aromatic Plant Sciences.* (1996). 18(4) : 788 - 790.

Uma, D.P., K. Akagi, *et. al. International Journal of Radiation Biology* , (1996). 69(2) : 193 - 197.

Yarden, A. and Lavie, D. Bull. Res. Counc. Isreal, (1962), Vol.11A (1), 35 - 36.

Withanolide - C — Withanolide present in *Withania somnifera.*

Bessalle. R and Lavie, D. *Phytochemistry*, (1992) Vol. 31 (10), 3648 - 3651.

Withanolide - D — Withanolide present in *Withania somnifera*.

Choudhary, K. and Neogy, R.K. *Biochem. Pharmacol.* (1975) Vol. 24(8), 919 - 920.; *Biol. Abstr.* 1975, 60, 62270.

Withanolide - C — Withanolide present in *Withania somnifera*.

Lavie, D.; *et. al.*, *Biol. Abstr.*, 1966, 3(18), 1275d.

Withanolide - Y — Withanolide present in *Withania somnifera*.

Bessalle. R., Lavie, D and Frolow.F., *Phytochemistry*, (1987) Vol. 26 (6), 1797 - 1800.

Withasomnine — Alkaloid present in *Withania somnifera*.

Morimoto, A., *et. al.*, *Tetrahedron Letters*, No. 54, 5707 - 5710.

Schroter, H.B. and Neumann, D. (1966), *Chem. Abstr.*, 1966, 65,170 - 15f.

90. SCOROPHULARIACEAE

Androsin — Glucoside present in *Picrorrhiza kurroa*. It is reported to be antioxidant.

Antirrhinoside — Glucoside present in *Antirrhinum majus*.

Apocynin — Glucoside present in *Picrorrhiza kurroa*.

Bacopasaponin - A — Dammarane-type saponin present in *Bacopa monniera*.

Garai, S., Mahato, S.B., Ohtani, K. and Yamasaki, K. *Phytochemistry* 1996; 42 : 815 - 820.

Garai, S., Mahato, S.B., Ohtani, K. and Yamasaki, K. *Phytochemistry* 1996; 43 : 447 - 449.

Bacopasaponin E and F — Dammarane-type saponin present in *Bacopa monniera*.

Mahato, S.B., Garai, S. and Chakravarty, A.K. *Phytochemistry* 2000. 53(6) : 711 - 4.

Bacoside - A — Steroid saponin present in *Bacopa monniera*.

Singh, H.K., *et. al.,*. *Phytotherapy Research* 1988; 2 : 70 - 75.

Bacoside - A_1 — Triterpenoid saponin present in *Bacopa monniera.*

Jain, P., Kulshreshtha, D.K., *Phytochemistry* 1993; 33: 449 - 451.

Bacoside - A_3 — Triterpenoid saponin present in *Bacopa monniera.*

Rastogi, S., Pal, R., Kulshreshtha, D.K. *Phytochemistry* 1994; 36: 133 - 137.

Bacoside - B — Steroid saponin present in *Bacopa monniera.*

Singh, H.K., *et. al., Phytotherapy Research* 1988; 2 : 70 - 75.

Boschnaloside — Iridoid glycoside present in *Euphrasia pectinata.*

Brahmine — Alkaloid present in *Bacopa monniera.*

Digitoxin — Cardiac glycoside present in *Digitalis purpurea.*

Digoxin — Cardiac glycoside present in *Digitalis purpurea.*

Euphroside — Iridoid glycoside present in *Euphrasia saliburgensis, Euphrasia officinalis* and *Euphrasia rostkoviana.*

Eurostoside — Iridoid glycoside present in *Euphrasia rostkoviana.*

Eukovoside — Iridoid glycoside present in *Euphrasia rostkoviana.*

Gitoxin — Cardiac glycoside present in *Digitalis purpurea.*

Herpestine — Alkaloid present in *Bacopa monniera.*

Ixoroside — Iridoid glycoside present in *Euphrasia stricta.*

Kutkin — Glucoside present in *Picrorrhiza kurroa.* It is reported to be hepatoprotective.

Kutki-sterol — Sterol present in *Picrorrhiza kurroa.*

Ladroside — Iridoid glycoside present in *Euphrasia rostkoviana.*

Leptandrin — Glucoside present in *Veronica virginica.*

Linarin — Glucoside present in *Antirrhinum majus.*

Mussaenoside — Iridoid glycoside present in *Euphrasia rostkoviana.*

Picrorhizin — Glucoside present in *Picrorrhiza kurroa.* It is reported to be hepatoprotective.

Thapsuine - A — Saponin present in *Verbascum thaspus.*

Thapsuine - B — Saponin present in *Verbascum thaspus.*

Veronicoside — Iridoid glycoside present in *Euphrasia rostkoviana.*

Verproside — Iridoïd glycoside present in *Euphrasia rostkoviana.*

91. BIGNONIACEAE

Baicalein — Flavone present in *Oroxylum indcium.*

Chrysin — Flavone present in *Oroxylum indcium.*

Oroxylin - A — Flavone present in *Oroxylum indcium.*

92. PEDIALACEAE

Harpagide — Glucoside present in *Harpagophytum procumbens.*

Harpagoside — Glucoside present in *Harpagophytum procumbens.*

Pedaline — Alkaloid present in *Pedalium murex.*

Procumbine — Glucoside present in *Harpagophytum procumbens.*

93. ACANTHACEAE

Acanthicifoline — Alkaloid present in *Acanthus ilicifolius.*

Acetylbarlerin — Glycoside present in *Barleria prionitis.*

Adhatodic acid — Acid principle present in *Adhatoda vasica.*

Adhatodine — Alkaloid present in *Adhatoda vasica.*

Allantoin — Alkaloid present in *Blepharis edulis.*

Andrographolide — Diterpene present in *Androgrpahis paniculata.*

Aphelandrine — Spermine alkaloid of *Aphelandra tetragona.*
Todorova, M. *et al.*, *Phytochemistry*, Vol. 37(5) : P. 1251 - 1256.

Blepharine — Alkaloid present in *Blepharis edulis.*

Callicarpone — Toxic principle present in *Callicarpa candicans.*

McChensey, J.D. *et al. J. Pharm. Sci.* 1979. 68(9) : 1116 - 20.

Callichiline — Alkaloid present in *Callichilia subsessilis.*

Justicin - A — Lignan present in *Justicia procumbens.* It is reported to be antiviral.

Asano, J. *et. al., Phytochemistry.* 1996. 42(3) : 713 - 7.

Justicin - B — Lignan present in *Justicia procumbens.* It is reported to be antiviral.

Asano, J. *et. al., Phytochemistry.* 1996. 42(3) : 713 - 7.

Justicidin - B8 — Coumarin present in *Justicia pectoralis.*

Justicin - C — Lignan present in *Justicia procumbens.* It is reported to be antiviral.

Asano, J. *et. al., Phytochemistry.* 1996. 42(3) : 713 - 7.

Justicin - D — Lignan present in *Justicia procumbens.* It is reported to be antiviral.

Asano, J. *et. al., Phytochemistry.* 1996. 42(3) : 713 - 7.

Kalmeghin — Diterpene present in *Androgrpahis paniculata.*

Neoandrographolide — Diterpene present in *Androgrpahis paniculata.*

Ouabain — Cardiac glycoside present in *Acocanthera ouabaio.*

Rhinocanthine — Alkaloid present in *Rhinocnthus nasuta.*

Swertisin — Coumarin present in *Justicia pectoralis.*

Tryptanthrin — Alkaloid present in *Strobilanthes cusia.* It is reported to be antimicrobial.

Honda, G., and M. Tabata. *Planta Med.* 36 : 85 - 90.

Umbelliferone — Coumarin present in *Justicia pectoralis.*

Vascinone — Alkaloid present in *Adhatoda vasica.*

Atta-Ur-Rahaman., *et.* al., *Natural Products Letters*, Vol. 10 - (4), 249 - 256.

Bhalla, H.L. *et. al.*, (1982), *Indian Drugs*, Vol. 20, pp.16.

Lakshmi, Poi, R.A. (1988). *J. Ind. Chem. Soc.*, Vol. 65(11), pp.814.

Vasicine — Alkaloid present in *Adhatoda vasica*. It is reported to be bronchodilator and abortifacient.

Atta-Ur-Rahaman., *et. al.*, *Natural Products Letters*, Vol. 10-(4), pp. 249 - 256.

Bhalla, H.L. *et al.*, *Indian drugs*, (1982) Vol. 20, pp. 16.

Chandoke, N., *Indian Drugs*, (1987) Vol. 24 (9), pp. 425 - 429.

Gupta, O.P. *et. al.*, *Indian J. Exp. Biol.*, Vol. 16(10), pp. 1075 - 1077.

Kannan, L.V. *et al.*, *Indian J. Pharm.* (1959) Vol. 21, pp. 108-109.

Vasicol — Alkaloid present in *Adhatoda vasica*.

Dhar, K.L., *et. al.*, *Phytochemsitry*, Vol. 20, pp. 319 - 321.

94. HIPPOCASTACASTANACEAE

Aescin — Glycoside present in *Aesculus hippocastacanum*.

Aesculin — Coumarin present in *Aesculus hippocastacanum*.

Fraxin — Coumarin present in *Aesculus hippocastacanum*.

Scopolin — Coumarin present in *Aesculus hippocastacanum*.

95. VERBENACEAE

Boucheoside — Iridoid glycoside present in *Bouchea fluminensis*.

Calliterpenone — Diterpene present in *Callicapra macrophylla*.

Camaraside — Flavonoid present in *Lantana camara*. It is reported to be cytotoxic.

Mahato, S.B. *et. al,. Tetrahedron* 1994, 50 : 9439 - 9446.

Castine — Bitter glucoside present in *Vitex agnus castus*.

Clerodin — Bitter glucoside present in *Clerodendron infortunatum*.

Durantoside - II — Iridoid glycoside present in *Bouchea fluminensis*.

Duranterectoside - C — Iridoid glycoside present in *Bouchea fluminensis.*

Lamiide — Iridoid glycoside present in *Bouchea fluminensis.*

Lamiidoside — Iridoid glycoside present in *Bouchea fluminensis.*

Lantanoside - A — Flavonoid present in *Lantana camara.* It is reported to be antimicrobial and cytotoxic.

Mahato, S.B. *et. al*, *Tetrahedron* (1994) 50 : 9439 - 9446.

Yuruker, *et. al. Pharmazie* (1995) 49(5) : 336 - 339.

96. BASELLACEAE

Clitorin — Flavonol glycoside of *Ullucus tuberosus.*

Fruechtel, J. and Welham, J.N. *Phytochemistry,* 55 (2000). 67.

97. LABIATAE

7 - acetoxymarrubiin — Diterpene present in *Ballota nigra.*

Seidel, V. *et al.* In : *PM* 62 (2) : 186 - 187. 1997.

Ajugalactone — Terpene present in *Ajuga reptens.*

Alboside - A — Iridoid glycoside present in *Pholmis tuberosa.*

Alboside - B — Iridoid glycoside present in *Pholmis tuberosa.*

Apigenin — Flavonoid present in *Scoparia dulcis.*

Cineole — Terpene present in the aromatic oil present in *Hyptis suaveolens.*

Copaene — Terpene present in the aromatic oil present in *Hyptis suaveolens.*

Dulcitol — Flavonoid present in *Scoparia dulcis.*

Excianin - A — Terpenoid present in *Rhabdosia excisa.*

Glechomafuran — Sesquiterpene present in *Glechoma hederacea.*

Glechomanolide — Sesquiterpene present in *Glechoma hederacea.*

Gluroside — Iridoid glycoside present in *Galeopsis tetrahit.*

Sticher, O. and Weisfloq, A. *Pharm. Acta. Helv.* 1975; 50(11) : 394 - 403.

Halosaline — Alkaloid present in *Haloxylon recurvum.*

Haloxine — Alkaloid present in *Haloxylon recurvum.*

Forskolin — Diterpene present in *Coleus forskohli.*

Forsythoside - B — Iridoid glycoside present in *Pholmis tuberosa.*

Lamalbide — Iridoid glycoside present in *Lamium album*

Menthol — Terpene present in *Mentha spicata* and other species of genera Mentha. It is antiseptic, antispasmodic and carminative.

Marrubiin — Glucoside present in *Marrubium vulgare.*

Nepetalactone — Terpene present in *Nepeta cataria.*

Ursolic acid — Diterpene present in *Ocimum sanctum.*

Picrosalvin — Diterpene present in *Rosmarinus officinalis.*

Rosmarinic acid — Diterpene present in *Rosmarinus officinalis.*

Scoparol — Flavonoid present in *Scoparia dulcis.*

Scutellarein — Flavonoid present in *Scoparia dulcis.*

Thujone — Terpene present in the aromatic oil present in *Salvia officinalis.*

Thymol — Sesquiterpene present in *Thymus vulgaris.*

98. ELAEAGNACEAE

Costunolide — Sesquiterpene lactone present in *Eremanthus elegnus.*

Eremanthin — Sesquiterpene lactone present in *Eremanthus elegnus.*

Laurenbiolide — Sesquiterpene lactone present in *Eremanthus elegnus.*

99. PLANTAGINACEAE

Acubin — Glucoside present in *Plantago ovata.*

100. NYCTAGINACEAE

Boeravinone A, B, C, C2, D, E — Rotenoids present in *Boerhaavia diffusa.*

Kadota, S. *et. al., Chemical & Pharmaceutical Bulletin,* Vol. 37(12), PP. 3214 - 3220.

Boeravine – Dihydroisofuranoxanthone present in *Boerhaavia diffusa.*

Ahmad, B. and Chung-Ping, Yu., *Phytochemistry,* (1992) Vol. 31 (12), 4382 - 4384.

Liriodendrin — Lignan present in *Boerhaavia diffusa.*

Pinitol — Glucoside present in *Bougainvillea spectabilis.* It is reported to be hypoglycemic.

Punarnavine — Alkaloid present in *Boerhaavia diffusa.* It is reported to be diuretic.

Agarwal, R.R. and Dutt, S. *Proc. U.P. Acad, Sci.,* (1935) Vol. 5, 240-242.

Punarnavoside — Glucoside present in *Boerhaavia diffusa.* It is reported to be antifibrinolytic.

Jain, G.K. and Khana, N.M., *Indian Journal of Chemistry,* (1989) Vol. 28B (2), 163 - 166.

101. AMARANTHACEAE

Ecdysterone — Saponin present in *Achyranthes bidentata.* It is reported to be anabolic.

102. CHENOPODIAEAE

Ascaridol — Terpene present in oil present in *Chenopodium ambrosoides.* It is anthelmintic and toxic.

Fagopyrin — Napthodianthrone present in *Fagopyrum esculenteum.*

Hyperoside — Flavonoid present in *Fagopyrum esculenteum.*

Oleragenoside — Glucoside present in *Spinacea oleracea.*

Pseudofagopyrin — Napthodianthrone present in *Fagopyrum esculenteum.*

Rutin — Flavonoid present in *Fagopyrum esculenteum.*

Salsoline — Alkaloid present in *Salsola kali.* It is reported to be antihypertensive.

103. DIPSACACEAE

Cantleyoside — Glucoside present in *Dipsacus sylvestris.*

104. WINTERACEAE

Drimenol — Sesquiterpene present in *Drimys winteri*

105. POLYGONACEAE

Chrysophanic acid — Anthaquinone present in *Rheum officinale.*

Dioscin — Saponin present in *Polygonatum zalanscianense.*

Lapathin — Anthaquinone present in *Rumex crispus.*

Polygonic acid — Acid principle present in *Polygonum aviculare.*

Rhein — Anthaquinone present in *Rheum officinale.*

Rheo - tannic acid — Tannin present in *Rheum officinale.*

Roseoside — Glucoside present in *Polygonum hydropiper.*

Murai, Y., *et. al., Planta Med.* 2001. 67(5) : 480 - 1.

Rumicin — Anthaquinone present in *Rumex crispus.*

106. ARISTOLOCHIACEAE

Aristolochene — Protein present in *Aristolochia indica.*

Aristilochine — Alkaloid present in *Aristolochia indica.*

Aristolochic acid — Bitter principle present in *Aristolochia indica.*

Chakranine — Alkaloid present in *Apama siliquosa.* It is similar to menispermine.

Ishwarone — Protein present in *Aristolochia indica.*

Ishwarane — Protein present in *Aristolochia indica.*

Isoaristolochic acid — Acid principle present in *Aristolochia indica.*

107. PIPERACE

Chavicin — Resin present in *Piper longum.*

Cubebic acid — Acid principle present in *Piper cubeba.*

Cubebin — Resin present in *Piper longum.*

Cubebol — Resin present in *Piper longum.*

Dihydrocubebin — Lignan present in *Piper guineense.*

Dwuma-Badu, *et. al., Lloydia* 38 : 343.9

Dihydropiperlonguminine — Delta ab-Amide present in *Piper guineense.*

Dwuma-Badu, D., *et. al., Phytochemistry* 15 : 822.

Kavaine — Alkaloid present in *Piper methysticum.*

Methysticin — Neutral principle present in *Piper methysticum.*

Piperine — Alkaloid present in *Piper longum.*

108. MYRISTIACEAE

Elemicin — Phenylpropanoid present in *Myristica fragrans.*

Myristicin — Phenylpropanoid present in *Myristica fragrans.*

Saffrole — Phenylpropanoid present in *Myristica fragrans.*

Titonine — Flavone present in *Virola michelli.* It is reported to be anti-inflammatory.

109. LAURACEAE

4 - O - methyl balophonin — Neolignan present in *Cassytha filiformis.*

Yuen, M. *et. al., J. Chin. Chem. Soc.,* Vol. 51, No. 1, 2004. 223.

Actinodaphnine — Aporphine alkaloid present in *Cassytha filiformis.*

Stevigny, C., *et. al. Planta Med.* 2002. 68(11) : 1042 - 4.

Bebeerine — Alkaloid present in *Nectandra rodiaei.*

Camphor — Terpene present in *Cinnamomum camphora.* It is antipruritic, antispetic and rubifacient.

Cassythine (= cassyfiline) — Aporphine alkaloid present in *Cassytha filiformis.* It is reported to be cytotoxic.

Stevigny, C. *et. al. Planta Med.* 2002. 68(11) : 1042 - 4.

Cassythidine — Aporphine alkaloid present in *Cassytha filiformis.*

Cassythine — Aporphine alkaloid present in *Cassytha filiformis.*

Cassyfromin — Neolignan present in *Cassytha filiformis.*

Yuen, M., *et. al., J. Chin. Chem. Soc.,* Vol. 51, No. 1, 2004. 223.

Dicentrine — Aporphine alkaloid present in *Cassytha filiformis.*

Stevigny, C. *et. al. Planta Med.* 2002. 68(11) : 1042 - 4.

Glaziovine — Proaporphine alkaloid present in *Ocotea glaziovii* (Lauraceae). It is reported to be antidepressant.

Marzo, A., *et. al., Eur. J. Clin. Pharmacol.* 1978. 31, 13(3) : 219 - 22.

Laurotetanine — Alkaloid present in *Litsoea grandiflora.* It is reported to be convulsant.

Megaphone — Ketone present in *Aniba megaphylla.*

S.M. Kupcham, *et. al., J. Org. Chem.* 43 (1987) 586.

Neolitsine — Aporphine alkaloid present in *Cassytha filiformis.* It is reported to be cytotoxic.

Stevigny, C. *et. al. Planta Med.* 2002. 68(11) : 1042 - 4.

110. LYTHERACEAE

Cryogenine — Quinolizidine alkaloid present in *Heimia salicifolia.*

Heimidine — Quinolizidine alkaloid present in *Heimia salicifolia.* It is reported to be anti-inflammatory.

Lythrine — Quinolizidine alkaloid present in *Heimia salicifolia.* It is reported to be diuretic.

Lythridine — Quinolizidine alkaloid present in *Heimia salicifolia.*

Lyfoline — Quinolizidine alkaloid present in *Heimia salicifolia.*

Nesodine — Quinolizidine alkaloid present in *Heimia salicifolia.* It is reported to be anti-inflammatory and antispasmodic.

Sinicuichine — Quinolizidine alkaloid present in *Heimia salicifolia* It is reported to be tranquiliser.

Vertine — Quinolizidine alkaloid present in *Heimia salicifolia.* It is reported to be anticholinergic, antiinflammatory, antispasmodic hyperglycemic, hypotensive, sedative, tranquilizer and vasodilator.

111. THYMELACEAE

Daphnane — Glucoside present in *Daphne mezereum.*

Dephnotoxin — Diterpene present in *Daphne mezereum.*

Mezerein — Diterpene present in *Daphne mezereum.*

112. LORANTHACEAE

Viscin — Lectin present in *Viscum album.* It is reported to be anticancer.

113. EUPHORBIACEAE

4 - methoxy – securinine — Alkaloid present in *Phyllantus amarus.*

4 - methoxy – norsecurinine — Alkaloid present in *Phyllantus amarus.*

Mulchandani, N.B. and Hassarajani, S.A., *Planta Medica*, (1984) Vol. 50 (1), pp. 104 - 105.

Acalyphine — Alkaloid present in *Acalypha indica*.

Amarin — Tannin present in *Phyllantus amarus*.

Foo, L.Y. (1992). *Phytochemistry*, Vol. 33 (2), pp. 487-491.

Amariinic acid — Ellagitannin present in *Phyllantus amarus*.

Foo, L.Y. (1992). *Phytochemistry*, Vol. 39 (1), pp. 217 - 224.

Baliospermin — Diterpenoid present in *Neoboutonia labrescens*.

Crotlorine — Dienone alkaloid present in *Croton bonplandianum*.

Crotonol — Resin present in *Croton tiglium*.

Cymol — Terpene present in aromatic oil present in *Euphorbia thymifolia*.

Carvacrol — Terpene present in aromatic oil present in *Euphorbia thymifolia*.

Crotosparinine — Proaporphine alkaloid present in *Croton bonplandianum*.

Euphorone — Ketone present in *Euphorbia tirucalli*.

Glochidionolide — Glucoside present in *Glochidion zeylanicum* (Euphorbiaceae).

Ostuka, H. *et. al.*, *Chem. Pharm. Bull* (Tokyo). 2003. 51(3) : 286 - 90.

Heliosin — Flavonoid present in *Euphorbia helioscopia*.

Chen, J.W., *et al.*, *Acta Pharmacol Sin*. 2002. 23(7) : 667- 72.

Y. Chen, *et. al.*, *Yao Hsueh Hsueh Pao*. 14, 91.1979.

Hypophyllanthin — Lignan present in *Phyllanthus niruri* and *Phyllanthus urinaria*. It is reported to be antiviral and cytotoxic. According to another study it lacks anticancer effect.

Row, L.R. *et. al.*, *Tetraherdon Letters* No. 24, pp.1557.

Somanabandhu, A. *et. al.*, *J. Nat. Prod.*, (1993) Vol. 56(2), pp. 233 - 239.

Srinivasalu, C., *Indian J. Pharm. Sci.*, (1992) Vol. 54(6), 253 - 54.

Isoeuphoral — Terpenic alcohol present in *Euphorbia tirucalli.*

Isolintetralin — Lignan of *Phyllanthus niruri.*

Huang, Y.L. *et. al.*, *Planta Medica*, (1992) Vol. 58 (5), 473 - 474.

Isorottlerin — Coloring matter present in *Mallotus philippinensis.*

Jatrophone — Diterpene present in *Jatropha isabellii* and *Jatropha grossidentata.* It is vasorelaxant.

Duarte, D.E. *et al.*, *Eur. J. Pharmacol.* 1992. 29; 215(1) : 75 - 81

Laudanidine — Alkaloid present in *Croton cryptocarya.* It is narcotic.

Limonine — Terpene present in aromatic oil present in *Euphorbia thymifolia.*

Montanin — Diterpene present in *Cunuria spruceana.* It is reported to be anticancer.

Gunsekera, S.P. *et. al.*, *J. Nat. Prod.* 1979. 42(6) : 658 - 62.

Nirphyllinn — Alkaloid present in *Phyllantus amarus.*

Nirurin — Flavanone glycoside of *Phyllanthus niruri.*

Gupta, D.R. and Ahmed, B. (1984), *J. Nat. Prod.* Vol. 47(6): 958 - 963.

Salicylic acid — Acid principle present in fixed oil present in *Euphorbia thymifolia.*

Sparsifoline — Alkaloid present in *Croton sprasiflora.*

Chatterjee, A. *et. al.*, *Tetrahedron Lett.* 1965. 21 : 1539 - 44.

Spruceanol — Diterpene present in *Cunuria spruceana.* It is reported to be anticancer.

Gunsekera, S.P., *et al.*, *J. Nat. Prod.* 1979. 42(6) : 658 - 62.

T - crotonin — Nor-clerodane diterpene of *Croton cajucara.* It is reported to be antiulcerogenic.

Tirucallol — Flavonoid present in *Euphorbia tirucalli.*

Transphytol — Present in *Phyllanthus niruri.*

Singh, B., *et. al., Planta Medica,* (1991) Vol. 57 (1), pp. 98

Ricin — Lectin present in *Ricinus communis.*

Ricinine — Alkaloid present in *Ricinus communis.*

Rottlerin — Coloring matter present in *Mallotus phillipinensis.*

Phyllanthin — Lignan present in *Phyllanthus niruri* and *Phyllanthus urinaria.* It is reported to be antiviral and cytotoxic. According to some authors it lacks anticancer effect.

Row, L.R. *et. al., Tetraherdon,* (1967) Vol. 23, pp.1915 - 1918.

Row, L.R. *et. al., Tetraherdon,* (1996) Vol. 22, pp. 2899 - 2908.

Somanabandhu, A. *et. al., J. Nat. Prod,* (1993) Vol. 56(2), pp. 233 - 239.

Srinivasalu, C. *Indian J. Pharm. Sci.,* (1992) Vol. 54 (6), pp. 253 - 54.

Phyllanthusiin - D — Tannin present in *Phyllantus amarus.*

Foo, L.Y. and Wong, H. *Phytochemsitry,* (1992) Volume 31(2), pp. 711 - 713.

Phyllantine — Alkaloid present in *Phyllanthus emblica.*

Phyllantidine — Alkaloid present in *Phyllanthus emblica.*

Phyllnirurin — Alkaloid present in *Phyllantus amarus.*

Pinitol — Flavonoid present in *Euphorbia esula.*

114. URTICACIAE

Divanillyltetrahyrofuran — Lignan present in *Urtica dioica.*

Triffydin — Toxic principle present in *Urtica ferox.*

115. MORACEAE

Bengalenoside — Glucoside present in *Ficus bengalensis.* It is reported to be hypoglycemic.

Augusti, K.T., *Indian J. Physiol Pharmacol.* 1975. 19(4) : 218 - 20.

Ficin (Fiacin) — Enzyme present in *Ficus glabrata* and resembles with papain. It is reported to be anthelmintic and toxic in higher doses.

Periplocymarin — Cardiac glycoside present in *Castilloa elastica* (Moraceae).

Adams, G.R. and Willkinson, S. *J. Pharm Pharmacol*. 1961. 13 : 279 - 82.

Psoralen — Furanocoumarin present in *Ficus hispida*.

116. JUGLANDACEAE

Juglone — Napthoquinone present in *Juglans nigra*. It is reported to be sedative.

117. BETULACEAE

Betulinic acid — Triterpene present in *Betula utilis*.

Leucoanthocyanidin — Proanthocyanidin present in *Betula utilis*.

Leucocyanidin — Proanthocyanidin present in *Betula utilis*.

Lupeol — Flavonoid present in *Betula utilis*.

Oleanilic acid — Triterpene present in *Betula utilis*.

118. SALICACEAE

Salicin — Glucoside present in *Salix tetrasperma* and *Salix capera*. It is antipyretic and anti-inflammatory.

119. HIPPOCRATEACEAE

Dulcitol — Xanthone present in *Salacia chinensis*.

Isoquesterin - A — Xanthone present in *Salacia madagascarinesis*. It is reported to be antileukemic and antiprotozoal.

Mangiferin — Xanthone present in *Salacia chinensis*.

Salacinol — Xanthone present in *Salacia chinensis*. It is reported to be hypoglycemic.

120. CANNABINACEAE

Cannabine — Alkaloid present in *Cannabis indica.*

Cannabisativine — Alkaloid present in *Cannabis sativa.*
Lotter, H.L., *et. al.*, *Tetrahedron Lett.* 33 : 2815.

Lupulin — Bitter principle present in *Humulus lupulus.*

Tetrahydrocannabinol — Resin present in *Cannabis indica.*

121. MYRICACEAE

Myricitrin — Glucoside present in *Myrica nagi.*

122. SMILACEAE

Parillin — Glucoside present in *Smilax officinalis.*

123. ORCHIDACEAE

Jebantine — Alkaloid present in *Dendrobium macraei.*

Loroglossin — Alkaloid present in *Orchis latifolia.*

124. ZINGIBERACEAE

Alpinin — Flavonoid present in *Alpinia galangal.*

Curcumin — Coloring matter present in *Curcuma longa.*

Galangin — Flavonoid present in *Alpinia galangal.*

Gingerol — Pungent compound present in *Zingiber officinale.*

Kaempferide — Flavonoid present in *Alpinia galangal.*

Shogoal — Pungent compound present in *Zingiber officinale.*

Zingiberene — Terpene present in volatile oil present in *Zingiber officinale.*

Zingiberol — Terpene present in volatile oil present in *Zingiber officinale.*

125. IRIDACEAE

Crocin — Apocarotenoid glucoside present in *Crocus sativus.*

Irosolidone — Flavonoid present in *Iris versicolor.*

Irosolone — Flavonoid present in *Iris versicolor.*

Picrocrocin — Bitter principle present in *Crocus sativus.*

126. AMAYRLLIDACAE

Acetylcaranine — Alkaloid present in *Ammocharis coranica.*

Ambelline — Alkaloid present in *Crinum latifolium.*

Assoanine — Alkaloid present in *Narcicuss assoanus.*

Flippin, L.J., *Org. Chem.* 59(1994) 3497.

Buphanine — Alkaloid present in *Boophone disticha.*

Caranine — Alkaloid present in *Ammocharis coranica.*

Crinamine — Alkaloid present in *Ammocharis coranica.*

Cliviine — Alkaloid present in *Clivia minita.*

Crinine — Alkaloid present in *Crinum asiaticum.*

Crinamine — Alkaloid present in *Crinum asiaticum.*

Crinidine — Alkaloid present in *Crinum giganteum.*

Crinosine — Alkaloid present in *Crinum giganteum.*

Epigalanthamine — Alkaloid present in *Lycoris radiata.*

Galantamine — Alkaloid present in *Galanthus nivalis.* It is cholinesterase inhibitor.

Glaucine — Alkaloid present in *Glaucinum flavum.* It is reported to be antitussive, anti-inflammatory and bronchodilator.

Alieshinskaya, E.E., *Pharmaceutical Chemistry Journal.* 1976 Jan.; 10(1) : 134 - 136.

Constant, O., *et. al. Thorax*, Vol. 38, 537 - 542.

Cortijo, J. *et. al., Br. L. Pharmacol.* 1999. 127(7) : 1641 - 45.

Haemanthidine.— Alkaloid present in *Haemanthus coccineus.*

Haemanthamine — Alkaloid present in *Haemanthus coccineus.*

Hippeastrine — Alkaloid present in *Lycoris radiata.*

Homolycorine — Amaryllidacene alkaloid present in *Narcissus pseudonarcissus.*

Lycoramine — Alkaloid present in *Lycoris radiata.*

Lycorenine — Alkaloid present in *Lycoris radiata.*

Miyasaka, K., *et. al., Jpn. J. Pharmacol.* 1979. 29(4) : 605 - 22.

Lycoricidine — Alkaloid present in *Lycoris radiata.*

Masonine — Amaryllidacene alkaloid present in *Narcissus pseudonarcissus.*

Narwedine — Alkaloid present in *Lycoris radiata.*

Norbelladine — Alkaloid present in *Hypoxis hirsute.*

Norpluviine — Alkaloid present in *Hypoxis hirsute.*

Powelline — Alkaloid present in *Crinum asiacticum.*

Ali, A.A., *Planta Med.* 1976. 30(4) : 369 - 74.

Pseudolycorine — Alkaloid present in *Lycoris radiata.*

Pretazettine — Alkaloid present in *Lycoris radiata.*

Scillaine — Glycoside present in *Galanthus nivalis.*

Scopoletin — Coumarin of *Solanum lyratum.* It is reported to be hepatoprotective.

Kang, S.Y. *et. al., Archives of Pharmacol Research,* Vol. 21(6) : 718 - 722, 1998.

Tazettine — Alkaloid present in *Lycoris radiata.*

Tortuosine — Alkalloid present in *Narcicuss tortuosus.*

127. HYDROPHYLLACEAE

Chysoeriodictyol — Flavonoid present in *Eridictyon californicum.*.

Eriodicytonin — Flavonoid present in *Eridictyon californicum.*

Eriodicytol — Flavonoid present in *Eridictyon californicum.*

Xanthoeriodictyol — Flavonoid present in *Eridictyon californicum.*

128. LILIACEAE

Ajoene — Terpene present in *Allium sativum.* It is reported to be anti-platelet.

Allicin — Terpene present in *Allium sativum.* It is reported to be hypolipidemic.

Alliin — Terpene present in *Allium sativum.*

Aloin — Bitter glucoside present in *Aloe vera.*

Asparagamine - A — Polycyclic alkaloid present in *Asparagus officinalis.*

Sekine, T., *et. al. Chem. Pharm. Bull.*, Vol. 4(6) : pp. 1360 - 1362.

Asparagoside - A — Steroid saponin present in *Asparagus officinalis.* It is reported to be cytotoxic.

Shao, Y., *et. al.* In : *PM* 63(3) : 258 - 262.(1997.)

Asparagoside - B — Steroid saponin present in *Asparagus officinalis.* It is reported to be cytotoxic.

Shao, Y., *et. al.* In : *PM* 63(3) : 258 - 262.(1997.)

Asparagoside - C — Steroid saponin present in *Asparagus officinalis.* It is reported to be cytotoxic.

Shao, Y., *et. a*l., In : *PM* 63(3) : 258 - 262.(1997.)

Asparagoside - D — Steroid saponin present in *Asparagus officinalis.* It is reported to be cytotoxic.

Asparagoside - E — Steroid saponin present in *Asparagus officinalis.* It is reported to be cytotoxic.

Shao, Y., *et al.,* In : *PM* 63(3) : 258 - 262. (1997.)

Aspartic saponin — Bitter saponin present in *Asparagus officinalis.*

Cholcamine (demecolcine) — Alkaloid present in *Colchicum autmnale*. It is reported to be antineoplastic.

Colchicine — Alkaloid present in *Colchicum luteum* and *Gloriosa superba*. It is anti-gout.

Colchicoside — Tropane alkaloid present in *Colchicum autumnale.*

Ulrichova, J., *et. al.* In : *PM* 59(29) : 144. (1993.)

Convallamarin — Cardiac glycoside present in *Convallaria majalis.*

Convallarin — Cardiac glycoside present in *Convallaria majalis.*

Convallotoxin — Cardiac glycoside present in *Convallaria majalis.* It is reported to be cardio active.

SH Lin., *et. al.*, 1980 1(2) : 100 - 104. Abstract.

Crocin — Apocarotinoid glycoside present in *Crocus sativus.* It is reported to be antioxidant, anticancer, antidepressant and heaptoprotective.

Escribano, J., et. al., Cancer Lett. 1996. 27; 100(1-2) : 23 - 30.

H. Hosseinzadeh, G. Karimi and M. Niapoor. *ISHS Acta Horticulturae* 650 : *I International Symposium on Saffron Biology and Bio-technology.*

Hossein, H., *et al.*, *J. Pharm. Pharmaceut Sci.* 8(3) : 387 - 393, (2005.)

Lin, J.K., Wang, C.J. *Carcinogenesis* 1986, 7 : 595 - 599.

Ríos, J.L., *et. al.*, *Phytother Res.* 1996, 10 : 189 - 193.

Disogenin — Steroid saponin present in *Asparagus racemosus.*

Subramanian, S.S. and Nair, A.G.R., *Curr. Sci.*, (1969) Vol. 38(17), PP. 414.

Eldrin — It is present in *Lolium philadelphicum.*

Euparone — Dibenzofuran present in *Ruscus aculeatus.*

ElSohly, M.A., *et. al.*, *J. Pharm. Sci.* 63 : 1623.

Ilixanthin — It is present in *Lolium philadelphicum.*

Imperealine — Alkaloid present in *Fritllaria pallidiflora.*

Li, S.L., *et. al.*, *Yao Xue Xue Bao.* 2001. 36(4) : 300 - 2.

Luteicine — Alkaloid present in *Merendera ramond.*

Timbekov, E. and Sadykov, A.S., *Chemistry of Natural Compounds*. 1985. 21(1) : 1 - 9.

Luteidine — Alkaloid present in *Colchicum richii*. It is reported to be cardiac tonic.

Ghisalbertii, E.L., *et. al.*, *Pharmaceutical Biology*, 1998. 36(4) : 237 - 239.

Phytomelin — It is present in *Lolium philadelphicum*.

Oxypinnatanine — Alkaloid present in *Hemerocallis fulva*.

Kruger, J.S., *et. al.*, *Journal present in South African Institute*, 1976, 29, 24.

Wang, Q., *et. al.*, *Zhongcaoyao*, 1990, 21.12.

Paridin — Saponin present in *Paris quadrifolia*.

Paristyphnin — Saponin present in *Paris quadrifolia*.

Pennogenin — Saponin present in *Paris quadrifolia*.

Peripalloside — Cardiac glycoside present in *Convallaria majalis*.

Phytomelin — It is present in *Lolium philadelphicum*.

Picrocrocin — Bitter glycoside present in *Crocus sativus*. It is reported to be anticancer.

Escribano, J., *et. al.*, *Cancer Lett.* 1996. 27; 100(1-2) : 23 - 30.

Ruscodibenzuran — Dibenzofuran present in *Ruscus aculaeatus*.

M.A. ElSohly, *et. al.*, *Tetrahedron* 33 : 17 – 11.

Safranal — Carotenoid present in *Crocus sativus*. It is reported to be antioxidant, antidepressant and chemo. preventive.

Fikrat, I. Abdullaev. *Experimental Biology* and *Medicine* 227 : 20-25 (2002).

H. Hosseinzadeh *et. al.*, *ISHS Acta Horticulturae* 650 : I. International Symposium on Saffron Biology and Biotechnology.

Hossein Hosseinzadeh and Hamid R. Sadeghnia. *J. Pharm. Pharmaceut Sci.* 8(3) : 394 - 399, (2005.)

Jorgensen, U., M. Hanson, *et. al.* (2000). *J. Agric. Food Chem.* 48(6) : 2376 - 2383

Spargin — Bitter principle present in *Asparagus officinalis.*

Shatavarin – 1 — Saponin present in *Asparagus officinalis.* It is reportd to be antiabortifacient.

Joshi, J.D.S., 1988. *Indian Journal of Chemistry Section B Organic Chemistry Including Medicinal Chemistry,* 27(1) : 12-16.

Shatavarin – 2 — Saponin present in *Asparagus officinalis.*

Shatavarin – 3 — Saponin present in *Asparagus officinalis.*

Shatavarin – 4 — Saponin present in *Asparagus officinalis.* It is reportd to be anxiolytic.

Superbine — Alkaloid present in *Gloriosa superba.*

Trilline — Saponin present in *Trillium erectum.*

129. PALMACEAE

Arecaine — Alkaloid present in *Areca catechu.*

Arecoline — Alkaloid present in *Areca catechu.* It is anthelmintic.

Guvacine — Alkaloid present in *Areca catechu.*

130. DIOSCOREACEAE

Diosbulbinoside – D — Norditerpene gluocoside present in *Dioscorea bulbifera.*

Diosbulbinoside – F — Norditerpene gluocoside present in *Dioscorea bulbifera.*

Diosbulbin – B — Norditerpene gluocoside present in *Dioscorea bulbifera.*

Diosbulbin – D — Norditerpene gluocoside present in *Dioscorea bulbifera.*

Dioscorin — Protein present in *Dioscorea batatas.* It is antioxidant, carbonic anhydrase and trypsin inhibitor.

Dioscin — Saponin present in *Dioscorea villosa* and *Polygonatum zalanscianense.*

Dioscorine — Alkaloid present in *Dioscorea hispida.*

Prazerigenin — Steroid saponin present in *Dioscorea prazeri.*

131. ACORACEAE

Acoretin — Resin present in *Acorus calamus.*

Acorine — Alkaloid present in *Acorus calamus.*

Asarone — Terpene present in *Acorus calamus.* It is reported to be carcinogenic.

Calamine — Alkaloid present in *Acorus calamus.*

132. POACEAE

Avenin — Protein present in *Avena sativa.*

Avenalin — Protein present in *Avena sativa.*

Citrol — Terpene present in essential oil present in *Andropogon muricatus.*

Coixenolide — Active constituent present in *Coix bacryma-jobi.* It is reported to be antitumor, analgesic, antipyretic and sedative.

Eleagnine — Alkaloid present in *Arundo donax.* It is reported to be antibacterial.

Gliadin — Protein present in *Avena sativa.*

133. JUNCACEAE

Juncusol — Phenol present in *Juncus roemerianus.* It is toxic.

134. EUPOMATACEAE

Lanuginosine — Alkaloid present in *Eupomatia laurina.*

135. OCHNACEAE

Calodenin - B — Bioflavonoid present in *Ochna macrocalyx.*

Trans - dihyrdocalodenin - B — Bioflavonoid present in *Ochna macrocalyx.*

136. THERMOPSIDEAE

Cystisine — Alkaloid present in *Thermopsis alterniflora.* It acts like nicotine.

137. CYNOMORIACEAE

Ursolic acid — Triterpene present in *Cynomorium songaricum.* It is reported to be immunodeficiency viral protease inhibitor.

Chaomei, *et. al.*, *Phytotherapy. Res.* (1998) 12 Suppl. 138 - 142.

138. EUPTELACEAE

Eupteleogenin — Glycoside present in *Euptelea polandra.*

139. BUDDLEJACEAE

Nuxioside — Iridoid glycoside present in *Nuxia floribunda.*

Unedoside — Iridoid glycoside present in *Nuxia floribunda.*

Verbascoside — Iridoid glycoside present in *Nuxia floribunda and Nuxia oppositifolia.*

140. STEMONACEAE

Isotuberstrmonine — Alkaloid present in *Stemona tuberosa.*

Oxotuberstrmonine — Alkaloid present in *Stemona sessilifolia.*

Stemonine — Alkaloid present in *Stemona tuberosa.*

Stemonidine — Alkaloid present in *Stemona tuberosa.*

Sinostemonine — Alkaloid present in *Stemona tuberosa.*

Stenine — Alkaloid present in *Stemona japonica.*

Tuberstrmonine — Iridoid glycoside present in *Nuxia sessilifolia.*

141. PROTEACEAE

Darligene — Tropae alkaloid present in *Darlingia darlingiana.*

INDEX

PHYTOCHEMICALS

A

B

C

E

F

G

H

I

N

Q

R

S

T

U

X

Y

Z